SQUAT DIDDLEY

YOUNG WRITERS

LONDON SURREY
AND HERTFORDSHIRE

1993

First published in Great Britain in 1993 by
POETRY NOW
4 Hythegate, Werrington,
Peterborough, PE4 7ZP

Contents

The Daffodil	Adebola Alele	1
You're Weird	Noel Faucett	2
Midnight	Haneef Syed Khalid	3
Questions	Natasha Shukla	4
Nobody Writes a Poem About Me	Manal Karrat	5
The Four Seasons	Shane Wilks	6
A Midsummer Dream	Uche Nosegbe	7
Yellow	Kathryn Pope	8
The Old Grey Cat	Leah Carpenter	9
Our World	Gemma Miles	10
A Memory	Omar Khan	11
Spring	Asad Gitay	13
The Knife	Chris Griffiths	14
I Hate Writing Poems	Owais Kazmi	15
Venesa	Natasha Grujicic	16
Unicorn	Jason Onyeneke	18
The Daffodil	Noreen Kelly	19
Freedom	Nichola Luu	20
Come Unto	Lorna Jessie O'Meara	21
This is Just to Say	Barry Lauder	22
The Night I Heard My Brother Cry	Sarah Mash	23
My Love Poem	Amiee Brown	24
Tiger Tiger	Katie Gillett	25
My Parents	Julie Ann Parkinson	26
School Poem	Natalie Tong	27
Come Unto My	Michelle V Greenfield	28
Come Unto	Matthew Thirlwall	29
Strawberry Moon	Fred Bernard	30
Drugs on our Street	Joy Edeki	31
I Saw	Daniel Quirke	32
What I Saw	Noel Cooney	33
Listen to Your Heart	Nirali Patel	34
Glass in my Hand	Moybur Rahman	35
Of Bubbles Burst	Amanda Doidge	36

Pain From a Distance	Anja Webb Ingall	37
The Stalker	Alan Anderson	38
Telling a Black Kid the Facts of Life	Juneha Begum	39
War	Julia Michelle Nott	40
Changing Lesson	Ruth Jenner	41
Night Time	Rizwana Choudhury	42
My Brother Wayne	Sarah Jane Carpenter	43
The Little Dove	Natasha Carby	44
Nature	Katie English	45
Earth	Claire Wood	46
Snow	Emily Murphy	47
Pollution	Deborah McCarthy	48
The Future World	Chetna Pandya	49
Mr Bean	Bob Marley/Pineapple	50
Cats	Victoria McGorm	51
The Hunter	Sally Bradforth	52
The Cute Cat	Shultana Ali	53
The Spider and the Fly	Khaleda Khalique	54
Break Torture	Emily Bloomfield	55
Hair Cuts	Cassie Wright	56
Rainbow Eyes	Joanna Jarvis	57
The Heart of Birth	Sarah V York	58
Fishing	David Killick	59
Food	Craig Harrison	60
Why?	Laura Claire Liddaman	61
The Star	Shelley Hales	62
Starting School	Helen Gibney	63
Shopping Trolleys	Robert Sewell	64
Childhood Dreams	Sara Morland	65
Love	Jackie Hooper	66
Seasons	Carolyn Lee	67
Love Hurts	Joanne Adamson	68
The Headless Postman	Clare Louise Billins	69
Love and War - 1945	Sarah Beckett	70
Teddy in the Attic	Emma Bartlett	71
Farewell Forest	Tracey Shanks	72
The Silent Night	Sarah Standage	73

Released Hostage	Natalie Sillwood	74
The Pain Inside	Jessica Melchior	75
Freedom	Charifa Ensser	76
Spirit	Lilah Aziz	77
Opening Ceremony	Hannah Christine Victoria Metcalfe	78
School Dinners	Julia Khanom	79
Cutting Trees	Rimni Begum	80
Don't See	Cheryl Stevenson	81
Shetland Disaster	Belinda Sarfo	82
Recycle Guard Rap	Natasha Walker	83
Save Our Home	Amina Ceesay	84
Human Greed	Freeroza A S Patel	85
Pocket Money	Zaheera Y Munshi	86
Pollution	Laurna Gooding	87
The Whales	Sarah-Anne Veal	88
Pollution	Sumaiya Banu Chikhalia	89
Pollution	Tajinder Khunghara	90
Litter	Aleya Begum	91
Walking Home	Runa Patel	92
The Sun	Kate Pitt	93
Washing Accident	Kelly Price	94
My Friend Ria	Siobhan Marie Goddard	95
Sea Dreams	Sylvia Spence	96
Freedom	Barry K Clarke	97
School Dinners	Samantha Wright	98
The Hippopotamus	Jeffrey Foy	99
Life v Death	Simon Henderson	100
Bottoms Up	Martin Murray	101
Wonderland	Darren Jordan Pasley	102
A Dirty Pig	Kimberly Walker	103
Growing Old	Thomas Straker	104
Horses	Louisa McGill	105
Being a Bird	Vicky Cliff	106
My Greenhouse	William Fenton	107
The Fox and the Man	Jake Binnington	108
Things at Night	Chris White	109
Dreams	Peter J Bellamy	110

Night Poem	Michael Paul Gerrard	111
A Sleepless Night	Stephen Greatorex	112
My Nightmare	Matthew Hempel	113
Sleepless Night	Siraj Yusuf	114
The Nightmare	Matthew Turk	115
The Nightmare	Jason Chong	116
Alone	Alex Donaldson	117
The PSE Lesson	Peter Lewis	118
Dreaming	Michael Moreland	119
The Darkness of the Night	Alexander Rothwell	120
Nightmares	Liam Thomas Parmenter	121
The Sleepless Night	Ben Tompkins	122
The Class Room	Nicola Chalkley	123
The Riding Lesson	Jacqueline Locke	124
The Hunt	James Roc	125
Mister Frog	Sarah Louise Jarrett	126
My First Ture Romance	Nicola Exell	127
Man	Paul Cruickshank	128
Panda	Joanne Lilly	129
The Childhood Dream	Lindsey Magill	130
If I Had a Great Big Hamburger	Matthew Outterside	131
The Unforgivable Sin	Bob Barbour	132
The Homeless Girl	Verity Anne Buchanan	133
She Feels No Different	Helen Milbourn	134
The Polar Bear	Matthew Brooking	135
Tiger Tiger	Craig Champness	136
The Perfect Goodbye	Philippa Louise Carmichael	137
The Subway	Clare harrison	138
Closed for Good!	Anna Gifford	139
I Sit Beside the Fire and Think	Ian Allardyce	140
My First Day at School	Oliver Dodd	141
Stormy Thoughts	Chris Muscutt	142
Cyril the Centipede	Carlos Dunn	143
Food Food Food	John Malyon	144
The Mariner's Log	Onur Gilleard	145
Imagination	Michael Blakeburn	146

People	Simon Swift	147
No Limits	Michael Darke	148
The Death of the Soldier	Shaun Bennett	150
The Wind	Previn Jagutpal	151
Parody of the Ancient Mariner	Chris O'Doherty	152
The Ancient Cricketer	Philip J Christie	153
Anger	Megan Lewis	154
A Warm Summer's Evening	Nicola Eaves	155
In a World full of Televisions . . .	Jennifer Reynolds	156
The Boat Trip	Anujah Srinivasan	157
Green	Kelly Hepple	158
Writing a Poem	Elaine J Round	159
The First Nativity	Kate Gallon	160
Problems	Sadeem Alsaid	161
Innocence	Beatrice Holford	162
Together	Chantelle Marshall	163
Protection and Safety	Matthew Poole	164
Memories	Rachel Fuller	165
Young Child	Linda Hirons	166
Axl Rose	Lisa Wilde	167
The Harpy	James M Collett	168
Cry of the Whales	Amber C Lane	169
Dolphin's Joy	Nicola Rodger	170
Creature	Katie Marie Young	171
Sheep	Susan Lake	172
Old	Julian Clift	173
The Wood Hunter	Tom Dearsley	174
Golden Lemur	Alex Meade	175
Turtle	Richard Harvie	176
Travelling Home	Alex Sawyer	177
Child	Marie Adlam	178
Creature	John Richard Draysey	179
Squirrel	helen Jackson	180
A Hare	Harriet Earis	181
The Wolf	Simon Berry	182
The Boy	Katie Meade	183
Racing the Tide	Sally Paul	184

Creatures	Melanie Brough	185
The Cat	Elizabeth Barnett	186
The Little Creatures	Naomi Elizabeth Sadler	187
Creatures of the Night	Marion E McCabe	188
Girl in Bright Colours	Laura Bazley	189
Tiger	James Windless	190
The Beaver	Danny Ranger	191
Medusa	Tim Jones	192
Pigs	Claire Etherton	193
The Otter	Kerry Louise Hudson	194
Jack	Neal Roberts	195
A Riot	Louise Roberts	196
Rain Destruction	Que Lu	197
The Long Cold Autumn	Eve Jessica Elizabeth See	198
An Absent Friend	Christine Horton	199
The Mill	Wendy Knox	200
The Church	Elizabeth Darton	201
No One Cares	Dawn Rutherford	202
Child of '93	Sally-Ann Spencer	203
Wind	Stacey Higgs	204
What Man Has Marred	Mary Woodland	205
Bosnia	Sarah Ashton Bartlett	206
Time	Emma Phipps	207
Waiting for Death	Estelle Hornsby	208
Watching Them Waiting	Victoria Swaile	210
Watching and Waiting	Ann Marie Pollard	211
The Story of Life	Lucy Griffiths	212
Bubbles	Joanna Winterton	213
Clouds	Ellen Laura Morgan	214
Ending	Catherine Stevenson	215
A Place of Dreams	Lucy Guilford	216
My Place of Dreams	Sarah Purkis	217
Day to Night	Peter John Abbott	218
I Would Paint	Eleanor F Haigh	219
Caravan Holiday	Debra Prince	220
The Whale	Hannah Laws	221
Tongue Twisters	Lee John Browning	222
Death	Adili Muguro	223

The Woods   Clare Forder   224
My Bug   Lucy Taylor   225

The Daffodil

I was once a low life,
who lived in soil,
But now I'm beautiful,
and very loyal.

I live in the ground,
I wait till spring.
After all this time,
I'm such a small thing.

Spring is near,
What will I be,
A lily, a rose,
Let's wait and see.

I've grown a bit,
I'm getting taller,
A few day's later,
I was smaller.

Oh look at me,
I'm as beautiful as ever.
But will my beauty last forever,
Never.

Adebola Alele (12) North Westminster School

You're Weird

You're weird, he said
I said, I know
He said to me
Why do you walk like a pigeon
in the middle of the snow?
Why do you sing Pavarotti
in the middle of the Sock Shop?
Oh why, oh why do you embarrass me
in front of all my class?
Oh why do you think you are Superman
and try to jump through glass?
Oh why do I have to tell you the answers
to the easy questions?
Don't you know?
You're weird, he said
I said, I know.

Noel Faucett (13) North Westminster School

Midnight

Midnight there is no light
It's medium really that's why it's called midnight.
Everyone sleeps at midnight so does
The sun, there's only one face that hasn't
Had it's face washed it's called the moon.
The moon is the only pure white, lit up bulb
At midnight
It's almost daylight people start to wake up.
Midnight has retired.
There's only one powerful bulb up,
And that's the face which has washed
Its face, that's why it stands out so bright
It's the sun.
The day has almost gone and here comes
Midnight.

Haneef Syed Khalid (12) North Westminster School

Questions

Questions, questions,
What are questions?
Curiosity? Yes, curiosity.
Questions that people ask you.
Questions that you ask yourself.
What makes the grass green?
What is the Solar System?
How big is the Universe?
Why is there pollution in the air?
Why isn't the world at peace?
These are all questions that are asked.
Questions, questions.
Life is one big pile of questions.

Natasha Shukla (12) North Westminster School

Nobody Writes a Poem About Me

Nobody writes a poem about me
They would rather write about a tree
Or about the blue sky
Or a bird flying high
Or about the beautiful sea
But no-one writes a poem about me.

Manal Karrat (13) North Westminster School

The Four Seasons

Pollen in the air
Daffodils in a row, Spring is here.
Busy bees are buzzing around the
flower beds ready to make their honey.

The bright sun shines,
As it melts my ice-cream, and
people wearing sun glasses
walking down the street.

It is getting cold, and the wind blows.
As I walk down the street it whistles in the
windy air.

The white snowflakes drop
like little pieces of paper gliding down to the ground.
The snow covers the ground like a sheet of cotton wool.

Shane Wilks (12) North Westminster School

6

A Midsummer Dream

As I laid on the grass I heard the
Music of the wind rustling past
I wondered to myself
Does life just consist of wars and dying?
Why can't we have peace, be satisfied with ourselves.
I felt good.
Until youth strolled past me, but the
Memories of the dream I had before
Made me mellow in the thoughts of
Enchanted youngsters, making me
Realise how it is to be free.
Like an eagle.
Sailing through the air.
Drifting down as the wings of time
Run out, leaving me with memories,
Enchanting ones running free.
Awaking, I realised that I had just had
A Midsummer Dream.

Uche Nosegbe (12) North Westminster School

7

Yellow

Yellow is a buttercup
In the summer sun

Like ladies Easter bonnets
And leaves in autumn

Egg yolk is yellow
Flames are yellow and bright
Winter is not yellow and neither is the night.

Kathryn Pope (12) North Westminster School

The Old Grey Cat

The old grey cat sat on the roof top
The old grey cat watched a small bird hop
The old grey cat wished he could catch the bird
But the idea was very absurd.

The old grey cat was very cold
The old grey cat's fur was thin and old.
The old grey cat's muscles were weak
No longer will he spring or leap

The old grey cat's home was quite big
The old grey cat's mistress used to be able to dance a jig
The old grey cat was a great friend
It was said when his life came to an end.

Leah Carpenter (12) Aylwin School

Our World

Soon our world will come to an end
Soon we won't be able to help or mend.
This poor old planet helpless and dying
With all this rubbish, pollution and lying.

With these horrible people cutting down our trees
Killing beautiful creatures like tigers and bees
And if we don't help this world quickly and soon
There will be nothing left but the sun and the moon.

Next time you don't throw your rubbish away in the bin.
Think of it as a terrible sin.
So think of the pollution and the thick dirty air
And when your about to throw down your rubbish
Beware!

Gemma Miles (13) Aylwin School

A Memory

As my eyes wandered,
The cold hit me,
And left me.

A wave of warmth,
In the dead classroom,
A glance,
A smile.

A faint trace of friendship,
Of warmth,
Acceptance,
From a cold school,
A rose blossomed,

In the darkness,
A pinprick of light,
From an auburn haze,
To a casting glow,

A touch of blue,
On a white moat,
A hint of red,
On a pillow of tenderness,
In a canyon of hate,

But as quickly as it came,
A vision will fade,
A school-day memory,
Becoming another moment,
In time,
In space,
In a lonely life,

A memory to me,
As she will always be. . .

Omar Khan (16) Willowfield School

Spring

As the frost cracks up and slithers away,
As the birds start to chirp their melodious songs,
And as the sun regains it's power,
Spring has begun to triumph.

Warmth makes the blood bubble, and skin
sweat as we've left behind the winter troubles.
Do all kinds of activities, lie in the sun, have a
refreshing drink, or even lay down for forty winks.

Come back to your abode, happy, feeling fresh,
switch on the TV and find the world in a mess.
Wonder why it's still the same, every year, every month,
nothing seems to change,
apart from the excuses which become more lame.

Rapes in Bosnia, killings in Kashmir, famine in
Solmalia, everything's clear.
So why oh why isn't there action, stop all the
culprits, and all the factions.

When will humans realise their mistakes,
adding to the problem, no givings just takes.

All they want is to make a profit,
leaving the troubled in a coffin.

Don't they know they've got the wrong system,
running the world on capitalism.

Asad Gitay (16) Willowfield School

The Knife

Sharp as a razor,
Soft as a whisper,
Innocent as a baby,
Until it is picked up.

Chris Griffiths (15) Cardinal Wiseman School

I Hate Writing Poems

I hate writing poems
They always seem to fail
It feels like all my thoughts
Are locked up in a jail.

When I try to rhyme poems
They never seem to work
And everyone at school
Say that I'm er. . .stupid.

Everyone looks at me
As though I'm about to cry
If I forget to put a capital letter
At the beginning of a line.

I wish I could write poems
I try to so very hard
But I know that the windows on my
jail are most definitely barred.

Owais Kazmi (13) Cardinal Wiseman School

Venesa

I dreamt you,
       My darling friend.
Though, not in the shape
  You would be today.

  I saw your soul,
In your
       Childlike image.

  And I cannot remember,
The words we exchanged
  But, I remember the
       pretty thoughts,
which ran through my mind.

  It was as if,
You had never gone.
  And when I awoke,
The awareness came.

  Aware,
       You were the perfect friend.
The one who gave,
      limitless love,
  And I am ashamed,
For myself.

  Aware,
      I've been asleep so long,
For now I know,
  You're truly gone.
And, how much you mean to me,
  It's only now
       I really see.

I really see,
    The pain I've hid,
Under my subconscious lid.
    Although I've never mourned,
        For you,

Only Shed a tear or two.
    I know how much,
You'll always mean.
    And, I hope that You are,
Happy,
        Dear.

    My darling friend,
My darling,
        Sister.
    We've reached the end,
Too soon.
        I love you.

Natasha Grujicic (15) Cardinal Wiseman School

Unicorn

Unicorn, Unicorn,
why thee eat thy acorn
with your horn?
why thee eat the acorn
your golden horn on your head
me the only mortal to see
thou unicorn
white as snow
how should I know
to look for your white coat again
you must have come from heaven
what God could make such
an animal, what tools
and the cool
it took to make such an animal
unicorn, unicorn
why thee eat thy acorn?
why thy leave a star in the sky?
why thy leave earth and float
how did you live on earth
and what does the unicorn eat?
grass or animals? big or small?
what does thy unicorn eat
and why does unicorn horn
shine so light.

Jason Onyeneke (13) St Michael's School

The Daffodil

Oh daffodil,
you are so brill,
and grow up to your beauty.
You stand up to your name,
you have lots of fame.
Your colour bright,
awake in light,
asleep at night.

Petals soft,
stem so strong,
all so long.
Your roots in soil,
soft and warm.

You wait for sun or rain.
If just one you die away,
your petals crisp,
head down.
Then suddenly you're dead,
crying in your bed.
Goodbye now,
you pretty little thing.

Noreen Kelly (12) St Michael's School

Freedom

Wouldn't it be nice to have freedom,
Wouldn't it be nice to be free,
Wouldn't slaves like to have freedom,
Just like you do, and me.

We capture animals in cages and do not let them free,
We lock them up in the cages,
In a place we wouldn't like to be.

People fight with their lives to get freedom,
They fight with their lives to be freed,
But all we do is sit here saying 'Is there any need?'
'Yes,' is the answer,
Yes there is a need!

So, let's get the world moving!
Let's get all the people *Freed!*

Nichola Luu (12) St Michael's School

20

Come Unto

Come with me to the place to be
where the red birds sing and
green trees rattle and the blue
sea splashing and the wind blow's
in your face where you can
feel your silk and smell the
rose on the grass.

Come to the place where there is a
breeze. Lots of leaves lots of trees
lots of roses lots of bees
we can sit by the river and
put our feet in the river or even go
for a swim.
Please come to the place where there
is a breeze.

Come to the place called a beach
where your feet sink in the sand
ah the taste of salt from the sea
just come to the beach please.

Come to the place called London
there are lots off shops for you
to go in, just come to London.

Come with me to school today
I'll read you a book and
maybe we will play.
Just come with me to
school today.

Lorna Jessie O'Meara (12) St Michael's School

This is Just to Say

I have stolen some of
the apples
that were hanging
on your tree.

I gave
some to
my friend and
saved the rest for me!

I'm sorry if I
hurt your feelings
or upset the apple tree
I didn't mean to do it I've
only stolen
three!

Barry Lauder (12) St Michael's School

The Night I Heard My Brother Cry

The night I heard my brother cry was very odd,
Because of that I prayed to God,
I said 'Dear Lord please stop that crying from my brother,'
Then I said, 'Is he okay Mother?'
Mum said, 'Yes phew,'
I said, 'Phew,' too,
Mum said I could now go to bed,
'Good night,' were the last words she said.

Sarah Mash (13) St Michael's School

My Love Poem

Love is good,
Love is bad,
Love can even make you sad,
Love is everywhere, here and there,
Love is even in the air,
Love goes on for ever more,
Love someone, don't be a bore.

Amiee Brown (12) St Michael's School

Tiger Tiger

Tiger, tiger in the forests of the night,
Tiger, tiger burn's so bright,
Tiger, tiger always stares
Tiger, tiger stalks his pray
To have a dinner for the day.

Katie Gillett (12) St Michael's School

My Parents

My parents are loving and kind
Parents like mine are hard to find.
My parents are really good to me,
The best parents that ever could be.
They love me and look after me.
Even wake me up in the morning,
with a nice cup of tea.
They help and carefully guide me in life,
My dad loves my mum, he says she's a
lovely wife.
My mum thinks the world of my dad
This is why I will never be sad.

Julie Ann Parkinson (12) St Michael's School

School Poem

School is boring
Sometimes good
School is for working
School for you and me
School is for educating your big brain
So don't strain your brain
Spanish is hard, harder than I thought
So I go to the next class to the next class I go
Science in the yard
So I won't blow up the class
Sum's are easy
Sum's are hard
Sometimes for you but not for me
Stories are fun, for you and me
So there are
Scary stories and fairy stories
Supper time's here so it's eat eat eat
So I have an idea lets eat sweets.

Natalie Tong (12) St Michael's School

Come Unto My

Come unto my garden path
  Where we can dance all night long
Let me love you o lovely one
  So we can have such lovely fun.

Come unto my garden path
  To eat up all the home made food
So that we would love the night together
  And keep as long as we live.

Michelle V Greenfield (13) St Michael's School

Come Unto

This is to a women I rather like,
I want you to come so I can show you I'm right,
And purple for the queen of my heart,
And white that will make you feel right,
With the sun and sea crashing on the shore,
And with red wine,
You will certainly be sure,
And I certainly hope your bright to come,
For you're the queen of my heart.

After that day on the beach,
I'm sure your heart follows me,
I was right,
You are very bright,
And now I'm sure,
you Know I'm right
One day you might walk up the hill in white,
The white that makes you feel right,
So I'm very certain you'll turn up
And make me settle at night
I wish we could get our hearts together
And always end like stories do
And I'm sure we will,
So I'm sure we'll kiss again,
And I'm sure your kiss,
Will make me sleep again tonight.

Matthew Thirlwall (13) St Michael's School

Strawberry Moon

Come to my heaven's up above
Where we can sit on cloud's and
eat chocolate fudge
Yes eat our heart away
Love I say is like a strawberry moon
Which vibrates like a tropical sand
dancer in the nude.

Fred Bernard (13) St Michael's School

Drugs on our Street

The world has turned a failure
drugs along the street
The government don't really care and forget
what they see.

For children of all ages are walking down
a wicked street.
Teenagers, gangsters, mobsters too is this what
you were born to do? children, children
sniffing what they can find, the liquid
won't take this dangerous fluid out of their
bad minds, violence occurs every day but policemen
just don't care.

Violence occurs day to day and policemen
can't control them they just want to shoot
them and run for bad minded children do
just not care just to make their friends
know that their broke and kills an old lady
walking on the street they take her money
until she falls on her feet.

Children, children
listen to this rhyme
in case you commit an illegal crime
not because I want to win this prize
for your futures will end soon if you
don't stop your evilness or go to prison school
dope drug what do you need it for? all it does makes
you die for more!

Joy Edeki (12) St Michael's School

I Saw

I saw a little fury mouse running across the floor
I saw a lovely little hole into which ran this mouse
I saw a very unusual ball it was a triangle shape
I saw a round goal into this ball it went.

Daniel Quirke (13) St Michael's School

What I Saw

I saw a big star on fire
I saw a lion with a leopard's skin
I saw a square football
I saw a ghost in the mist
I saw a talking monkey
I saw a flying horse
Then I woke up from this magic dream.

Noel Cooney (12) St Michael's School

Listen to Your Heart

I am sitting here trying to express my thoughts,
My feelings that I cannot say.
My heart tells me that I love you
We spent so little time together,
But I feel like I spent years with you.
When I see a couple walking hand-in-hand I imagine
you near me.
You are always in my heart and in my soul.
You are a symphony a harmony,
A comedy and a play.
My respect for you is great,
My love for you is immense.
I must have spent hours looking at the sky,
And seeing your face smiling at me.
I have imagined you laying your head on my shoulder.
And if we were to cry we'd make wine from these tears.
You are my prayers, my dreams,
And all the steps that I take,
Friends say, 'He is not right for you,'
But I have a feeling which insists,
I listen only to my heart.

Nirali Patel (16) Fulham Cross School

Glass in my Hand

Now I have a glass in my hand
There's so much work to be done
If ever I find the time, I'll stop to think
I'll think about the world
Who dies before their birth?
And who cares about the dawn?
Who can fear the night of sorrow
When the evening is too delightful
I got a little tired
And mixed a little lie in
With the truth
I picked up a bottle and drank . . .
And felt so soothed within.

Moybur Rahman (17) South Camden Community School

35

Of Bubbles Burst

Searchingly my steely eyes, absorb the greeny blue.
Menacingly colliding sand, sea and sky.
Undulating the waves of blue, now purple mass,
Heaving to and fro, to and fro . . .
Shattered, my thoughts exercise the things they know.

Looking out across the sand, my grey matter ebbs and flows.
Decaying and drifting . . .
Tripping over some old dead wood
I kick it with my old brown boots.
Old time, old hope.

But walking on, I brace myself, against the steely smoky sky.
Wondering on my mental health.
I leave the crumbled remains of wood,
Scattered across the sand.
Soon to be washed away by sea and tide.

Meandering on my way through past, past pains and loves.
I slip through my man made abyss.
While floundering amongst the blueness
Of my monotonous memoir,
I watch the gulls as they circle and glide, blue grey against white.

I gasp with horror, as I watch life,
Through my blue tinted lenses.
Looking behind me all I see is
Billions of bubbles burst . . .
Once cared for and loved.

Nurtured, warmly gloved.
All have been savaged
Stolen and sold, by
Purple, green murderers . . .
Reality unknown alone, is the protector of bubbles unburst.

Amanda Doidge (16) Leyton Sixth Form College

Pain From a Distance

She looked at me
Anguish piercing blue eyes.
Slowly, silently a tear trickled down
Lines of beauty, distorted by tears.

Abundant clear rain
Dropped,
Blanketing smooth,
Unblemished cheeks.

Enveloped in black,
Unearthly, pale, whitewashed skin
Against dark lanks of hair.
A silhouette.

She was suffocated.
Swallowed by the mingling of dark and sadness.
A shawl draped fragile shoulders
that heaved with despair.

I watched her.
An island of anguish.
I cried in empathy,
For something I could not comprehend.

I was young, naive
But crying in unity,
Linked through fear,
I felt old.

Anja Webb Ingall (18) Leyton Sixth Form College

The Stalker

His black hair like the heart of the devil,
As he *Stealthily* moves at grass level,
His long tail like a *winding* stream,
As he gracefully moves like a child in a dream,
His teeth are like talons on a *lethal* claw,
Lined up in rows in a powerful jaw,
He moves *slowly*, close to the ground,
His feline body not making a sound,
The sweat on his back *sparkles* in the hot summer's day,
As slowly he stalks his unsuspecting prey,
He moves in, with *power* and skill,
As slowly he moves, in for the kill,
He studies his prey with bloodshot eyes,
His pupils like ponds *reflecting* the skies,
He moves ever closer, like a cat to a bird,
But slowly his prey moves back to its *herd*,
He *pursues* his prey and moves ever closer,
With fiery fury he leaps to injure or kill her,
His *vicious* claws hit the animal's side,
Ripping and tearing at the animal's hide,
So back to the kittens with the meat,
Another day's food for the *prowler* to eat.

Alan Anderson (14) Woolwich Polytechnic

Telling a Black Kid the Facts of Life

They see it as abnormal
If you've got a different colour skin.
They'll make you feel like it's the end of the world
When a few breaths ago you felt the beginning.
When you walk down the streets
they're disgraced by your face
they hate you without knowing you
because you're a different race.
Deep down the anger gets trapped
when their look displays so much hate
committed a crime from the day you were born
then was still too late.
When prejudice poisons one innocent mind
it works it's way through others
and together they're unkind.
They take away your self respect
their hate eats away any security
I've fought hard to break down the barriers they built
but instead they gave me a suppressed identity.
You'll live a life which is not your own
being around so many you'll be so alone
because they base their love on a certain colour
and we're guilty of being the wrong one
but our blood like theirs will always bleed red
we'll always feel hot under the sun.
Us and them have many things in common,
but still nothing we can do or have done
will change the colour of our skin
and their value of our life
no force is strong enough to fight this one.

Juneha Begum (17) Mulberry School For Girls

War

There was a minute of silence
For those we lost.
All those years ago.
The wreaths we laid
On the graves
Full of poppies and sadness.

People dressed in black.
With veils and hats
Stood in silence
While the cannons went *Boom!*

Remembering the days of,
blackouts, bombs, death and
the enemy.

Julia Michelle Nott (12) Enfield County School

Changing Lesson

Waiting in class for the buzzer to go.
One more minute then it will go.
Art next lesson great! I love art
The buzzer goes we all pack away.
Rushing to get to the classroom first.
Hoping you are not going to lose your way.
Everyone shouting you feel uneasy.
Finding your way is never easy.
Walking all those stairs is hard work
I wish I was there.
Another grey door could this be
The room I am looking for?
Oh! yes it says 'Art' on the door.
I get to my desk and look in my bag.
Get out my drawing pad and pencil.
I love art but I am getting hungry.
So I hope the next buzzer is for lunchtime.

Ruth Jenner (12) Enfield County School

Night Time

No golden sun in the blue sky.
In the sky, only the stars and moon
Highlighting the dark blue sky.
Gorgeous are the foxes and badgers
Time through the day has past
Only nocturnal animals are awake
Ingenious humans are fast asleep
As morning light is getting closer
Every street lamp's light starts to fade away.

Rizwana Choudhury (12) Enfield County School

My Brother Wayne

I have a brother called Wayne,
Who sometimes can be a pain,
He acts all macho but looks like a tacho,
His hair is all spiky,
And the girls say not likely,
He gets so upset,
And says, 'you don't know what your missing yet.'

Sarah Jane Carpenter (13) Enfield County School

The Little Dove

I know you little dove,
You're as pretty as can be.
I know if your in trouble,
So don't worry me.
I'll come and save you,
before you die.
So come on little dove,
Don't worry me.

Natasha Carby (12) Enfield County School

Nature

Nature, nature
Harbour nature
None of the animals
Do have beards
Nor are they in cages
They've all disappeared
From the yellow pages!

Katie English (12) Enfield County School

Earth

We live on a planet
Earth is the name
We spin around our bright hot sun,
Day in day out, till a year has gone.

But soon our planet,
Will come to an end
For the pollution in the air,
And the rain forests that have gone.

Now our planet earth is at an end,
For the earth has split in two,
Down we went,
Down the hole.

That happened because the people think about money,
not about the earth.
They chopped down rain forests,
Polluted the air, now the earth has gone.

Claire Wood (12) Enfield County School

Snow

it's morning
Snow begins to fall
And I give out a call
I run for my coat
My brother does too
And we both run outside
To play in the snow
it's so white and clean
Just like a dream
When you walk on the
snow your footprints appear
They stand out so clear
We throw snowballs
And build snowmen
Which look real in the dark
My dog barks
It's morning
And all that is left of our snowman
Is his hat and scarf
Which lie on the garden path.

Emily Murphy (12) Enfield County School

Pollution

We all use energy
That can cause pollution
Why can't we buy less things
Then factories don't have to
Make lots of things
So we can save a lot of energy
Without polluting the air.
So go down to the shops
And buy things that are
Ozone Friendly
And things that wouldn't
Pollute the air.

Deborah McCarthy (12) Enfield County School

The Future World

If we don't look after the world, we will destroy our planet.
No more trees, no more pets or wild animals
All we will have will be polluted air,
Factories that have big fat chimneys,
With greyish black clouds of smoke coming out the top.
Also no houses with nice beautiful gardens or any sort of plants.
That is only some of the things that will happen to the earth
if we don't look after it.
Maybe if we look after it now, then we could make our planet
a better place for all of us.

Chetna Pandya (12) Enfield County School

Mr Bean

I know a teacher
His name is Mr Bean
And he is very mean
He likes to shout
And boast about
We all jump
He gives us a clump
And gets the mumps
It comes to the end of school
He isn't cruel at all
We are getting on the bus
And Mr Bean is following us
We have another mile for Mr Bean to smile
We are finally there
When he starts to care
he gives us a huge hug
He starts to talk while he starts to walk
We become good friends when it finally ends.
I'm sorry to say
I have to go for today
See you tomorrow in class 7A.

Bob Marley/Pineapple (13) Enfield County School

Cats

During the day
cats are nice cats are cute.
Cats are tame and never get the blame.
But during the night it's not the same.
During the night cats get the blame if a dustbin bag is ripped
Or if the gold fish is missing.
During the night cats are vicious and wild.
They're looking for a fight
And after that with blood dripping down,
They're looking for a bite, a mouse or a rat,
Or a bird that's asleep in a tree.
They would be so quiet on their soft padded feet
You wouldn't hear a low rustle or a purr until
Snap a nice juicy rat.
But the cat would not be greedy
The cat would take it home for his owner
in the morning to find at his feet.
And then the cat will purr happily
When it gets a pat on the back and told 'good cat.'

Victoria McGorm (12) Enfield County School

The Hunter

As she glides through the grass,
Stalking her prey,
She is as quiet as the mouse,
She is stalking.

Suddenly she pounces . . .
. . . and misses,
But she just pretends,
That she was playing,
With the dead leaves.

As she slinks around,
Her silky coat shines,
In the moonlight.
But when day comes,
She is a different cat,
Altogether.

Loving, purry, the cat,
Who all the family,
Know and love.

Sally Bradforth (12) Enfield County School

The Cute Cat

I went to this sweet shop
And there I saw a cute cat
I couldn't stop starring at it
So I knelt down and started to tickle
Later all of a sudden he started to bite
And I started to scream.

Shultana Ali (12) Enfield County School

The Spider and the Fly

Where's the spider?
He's made his web wider
Where's the fly?
He's just passed by.

Khaleda Khalique (13) Enfield County School

Break Torture

The dreaded bell rings for the start of the day.
There's no turning back I'm here to stay.
The torture has started
Lesson after lesson
English first and maths second.

Minute by minute the clock ticks slowly,
With break on my mind I'm getting ready to go
Gazing at the time every second,
wishing that the hands will speedily go by
But finally the bell goes! (What a relief!)

The rush to get outside is horrific
The stamped of feet is reaching a crescendo!

Break
Thank goodness I am free.

Emily Bloomfield (14) Thamesmead School

Hair Cuts

When I have my hair cut my friends say:
    Oh you've had your hair cut
    Oh you should wear a hat
    Oh you've had a scare cut
    and silly things like that.

I can't stand having my hair cut
though I'd rather let it grow.
What I can't stand is being told
I've had it cut,
as if I didn't know.

Cassie Wright (14) Thamesmead School

Rainbow Eyes

Do my eyes not deceive?
Cascading colours before me.
Feelings, emotions cling to the colours,
Reason, explanation.

Do my eyes not deceive?
Colours can mean so many things,
Wrath, fire dancing deep within
A label stamped with *red*

Do my eyes not deceive?
A shower of colours before me.
Blue is a reflection, a trickling stream.
A shiver down my spine.

Do my eyes not deceive?
A fountain of colours before me
Yellow is, of course, blooming dandelions

Do my eyes not deceive?
Colours scattered upon the floor,
Black is mystery, the dead of night,
Merging shadows all around.

Do my eyes not deceive?
A fountain of blending shades,
floating down, into my rainbow eyes.

Joanna Jarvis (14) Thamesmead School

The Heart of Birth

You arrived
from a Celestial Lantern
of golden ivory
smothered in Chaste milk.
Cradled in the vault of heaven
through the breach of your sky.

    : Mother

with the dew of sentience
dripping off of her lashes
and a well of devotion
snuggled in her breast,
who breeds warmth
with a one-ray of
colour-collosul
spectacle - spectacular
    : which patterned you eternally.

Spreading her copious, octopus arms
She let you go

and seeing the final light
when you began to caress her
moist inside
and when your eye was half-open
    : the foetus stopped revolving
      around the womb.

Sarah V York (17) Woodhouse SFC School

Fishing

'The one that got away' is what the old sea dogs say.
The sport that turns boys into heroes and men into great
storytellers.
Walking down the river's edge with me rod in one hand, little
seat box , and frost bite in my fingers.
It's eight o'clock without a bite. I've been sitting here half
the night.
Come on little fish grab that hook, bend my rod and see me
fly to my reel or see me cry!
Bang! goes the rod top and off I go. 'I've got one!' I cry.
What is it, how big? then I got snagged on a bloody twig,
that fish ain't gonna get away even if I have to dive in.
'Hurrah' I shout with a gleam in my eye as the twig
comes away so I don't have to dive in.
Amazed as I get my first glimpse of a large Roach,
glimmering and gleaming under the water's surface as
the sun beams down on a brilliant swimming machine
Dad takes a photo of me and my machine, of course
I let it go to swim free again and bring a smile to another
hero's face.

David Killick (12) Thameside School

Food

Food we need,
Food we eat,
A baked potato,
A piece of meat,
Some baked beans,
Some chocolate cake,
Don't waste your food,
For goodness sake.
The homeless people,
Have no money,
Don't laugh at this poem,
It's not so funny.
People are starving,
Look at their faces,
Don't laugh and joke,
They're all over the places.
Just give a bit,
It's not so bad,
If we raise enough money,
People won't be so bad.

Craig Harrison (13) Thamesmead School

Why?

Why do I have to go to bed?
You don't go to bed till late.
Why can't I have some wine?
You drink it all the time.
Why can't I drive the car?
You drive all over the place
Why can't I watch the scary horror movies?
I won't be scared, I promise.
Please tell me why I can't do these things
Oh tell me please I beg
OK I might be a little small,
But I will eat my greens and grow.

Laura Claire Liddaman (13) Thamesmead School

The Star

There once was a girl,
Who sat upon the windowsill.
Every night she saw a star
shining bright,
I wonder why it shines so
bright up in the sky.
I wonder why,
I wonder why.

Maybe it is there to guide
you,
To help you on your way.
Side by side with other stars,
Shining bright,
Shining bright.
Now I know why,
now I know why.
It shines so bright up in the sky.

Shelley Hales (13) Thamesmead School

Starting School

Starting school is a new experience,
Trembling I go in the gate,
A teacher comes right up to me,
'Rachel,' she says to another girl,
'Take Katie to her classroom.'
I follow Rachel down the corridor,
Nervously I look round the door,
Great numbers of children sitting in rows.
Scared I go up to the front,
Choking, I stammer my name
Hoping the children won't laugh at me.
Out in the playground,
On the lookout for bullies,
Lonely till others come to play.

Helen Gibney (14) Thamesmead School

Shopping Trolleys

Shopping Trolleys are a stupid invention
what exactly is their intention?
Shopping trolleys are supposed to help you,
to make you glad,
but they make you angry,
they make you mad,
there're big, there're ugly, the wheels are too small,
they make you crash into the baked bean stall.
So next time you go shopping with your mum
or Aunt Polly,
remember the curse of the shopping trolley.

Robert Sewell (14) Thamesmead School

Childhood Dreams

When I was young, stars
Were made for wishing,
And every hole deep in a tree, hid a leprechaun.
Old houses all have secret rooms
If I could find a key,
The rooms which I dreamt of every night
Would belong to me.

'Grow up' the grown ups said.
'Someday you'll wake and find,
That these hopes are just childhood dreams,
You'll have to leave behind
Like clothes that will no longer fit
Or toys that you'll ignore.
You'll not believe in magic anymore.

My child sleepy in my arms,
Looking up at me
Looking deep into my eyes
I wonder what he sees?
Perhaps he knows about secret rooms
Or holes deep inside trees.
Maybe he thinks of the same magical things,
As his loving mother, *me.*

Sara Morland (15) Thamesmead School

Love

Love comes and goes
so fast,
Love you will find it and then
it leaves.
Love while it lasts
takes you as high as a kite.
Then it drops you right
back in the gutter.

Love is the light
of your life,
love is doom and
gloom,
Love is the thing
you need,
Then it breaks your heart.

Love nobody can live
without it,
Love nobody can live
with it,
Love is still an
unknown thing.

Jackie Hooper (15) Thamesmead School

Seasons

In the Spring
The sky is blue
The grass is green
During the day and through the night.
The trees are in bloom.
The world is everything.

In the Summer
The gardens are bright
As they sing in the daylight
Yellow, red, pink, blue
Are the flowers of you.
The world is everything.

In the Autumn
The trees shed their leaves
And they tumble down
Colours of brown, yellow and red
The world is everything.

In the Winter
The trees look dead
No leaves just branches
The bright gardens are dead
So the garden's bare.
Although there might be snow
The world is everything to us.

Carolyn Lee (15) Thamesmead School

Love Hurts

Our love is strong
it can't break up
can't break down.
It will always be around
our love is as deep as any ocean
It's made to last don't you know.
This love is strong.

We've been through the hard times
But through the rain shone the sun.
All it needs is trust.
The more that we're together.
Our love just gets better.
We both know it's true.
There's nothing to come between me and you.
This love is strong.

Joanne Adamson (15) Thamesmead School

The Headless Postman

The postman cycled down the road,
to see just one of his ladies.
He knocked on the door,
and went right in to discover, oh no . . . his wife.
He tried to form some kind of excuse,
but after a while gave in.
She marched over and grabbed his tie,
but then discovered he was about to die,
She loosened her grip, as was a violent lady,
and preferred the blood and gore.

She threw him in the car,
and drove to her castle,
Where she planned to chop off his head.
She'd always enjoyed beheading people,
and it was one of her greatest flairs.

The blade covered in blood and brains
the wood rotted and old.
She lay him down and tied his hands,
and walked over, to the wheel.
The wheel was already wound up so all she had to do,
was cut the rope and down the blade would fall,
She got her knife and began to saw,
at the rotted old rope.
It finally snapped and down went the blade,
Chopping his head off hooray - she shouted.

. . . if only life were this simple . . .
. . . and easy to get revenge.

Clare Louise Billins (13) Thamesmead School

Love and War - 1945

Battling through harsh, crashing waves.
Heading towards white iron cliffs.
Staring into a mask of death.
The sound of ringing gunfire splits and tears the air,
Burning shrapnel, darts enraged,
Ripping the sea, land and men alike.
Stumbling forwards, Germans perched high above like hovering
eagles,
Leering faces.
Deadly weapons fling an array of stinging agony.
Fighting for France and power.
Doubt flees replaced by anger,
Struggling onwards, barbaric and indignant.
A fountain of bullets cascade down,
Cutting off the world and the war . . .
Forever.

Tears of heartbreak splashed upon green velvet,
A respectful silence broken only by the surging sea.
Soldiers lie, side by side
As they once stood in combat.
Now resting, honoured forever.
A marble light, shining brightly
Allowing no-one to forget.
Ranks of warriors,
Queuing,
Waiting quietly
In eternal peace,.
Rows of guardian angels, standing solidly
Their arms held open protecting, sheltering the memories
Of valiant heroes.

Sarah Beckett (13) Thamesmead School

Teddy in the Attic

Teddy in the attic,
Dusty and old.
He's no longer used,
No longer bold.

He once lived a happy life,
Played with every day.
But now the child has grown up,
Married, and lives far away.

When the trap door opens,
Teddy's hopes are up.
'Will they bring me down?'
Bang! The trap door shuts.

Teddy in the attic,
One day he is found.
'Look it's my old teddy!' she says,
As he's swung round and round.

Emma Bartlett (13) Thamesmead School

Farewell Forest

Farewell forest, dark and dank,
Farewell otter on the riverbank,
Farewell badger, farewell mole,
From your deep and darkened hole,
Farewell birds up in the trees,
Farewell nest of buzzing bees,
Farewell eagle, farewell fox,
Soon to be kept in a ladies box,
Farewell mountains, farewell seas,
Loggers come to cut down trees,
Soon the forest withers and dies,
Then disappears from human eyes.

Tracey Shanks (16) Thamesmead School

The Silent Night

The sky darkens like curtains that
have been pulled.
The shining moon glittering way
up high,
sending down a florescent beam
of white clear light.
Stars like specks speckling the sky
for miles stretching to the limit all
over the world.
Everything is silently quiet,
the whispering of the trees swaying
gently in rhythm with the sound.
A faint howl of a fox on his nightly prowl.
The evil come out tonight.
Ghosts, spirits - but it's all a fake.
I can picture people, resting, sleeping
dreaming of their wonders, ambitions
and dreams.
Although many hard workers still
using the night for our safety
People like fire-fighters, policemen and
nurses awake to make a pleasant
Silent Night,

Sarah Standage (13) Thamesmead School

Released Hostage

The moment I stepped out of the slum I had lived in for so long,
I knew I would remember it for the rest of my life.
I was free at last.
I inhaled a long awaited breath of cool, fresh air,
So different from the stuffy atmosphere of the prison I had left
behind.
I stood there for a while just surveying the scene around me.
I used to think that the same area looked dull and bleak,
But that day it was paradise.
Everything looked so tranquil and calm,
As though nobody had a care in the world.
The way I was before.
A passing couple smiled and greeted me as they walked along,
I returned the gesture, pleased that someone had noticed me.
I was someone again.
Not someone's property.

Natalie Sillwood (14) Thamesmead School

The Pain Inside

All very quickly I fell to the ground
All very sudden with a great big bang
As I lie there as still as I could be
I felt a hand touching me
I tried to run, but it was too late
I heard him whisper something about my fate
As his fingers slid into the curls of my hair
I caught a glimpse of his terrible stare
His fingers grew tight pulling my head off the floor
Somehow I knew this could go on no more
I tried to pretend the pain would go away
But somehow I knew it was here to stay
Although by bruises may soon be gone
And cuts and scars won't stay for long
But I know the one thing that will stay
And that's the one thing that won't go away
It's pain and hate that stays inside
And that's the one thing I just can't hide.

Jessica Melchior (15) Thamesmead School

Freedom

I wish I was free like a bird
in the sky,
Flying up, there so high,
Watching all the people go by.
I am so free,
I could cry.

Charifa Ensser (13) St Augustine School

Spirit

If my spirit was free,
I would be the sea,
Rough and exciting,
Soft and calm,
A mixture of feelings
So if my spirit was free,
I would only be the beautiful sea.

Lilah Aziz (12) St Augustine School

Opening Ceremony

A dressage of Colour,
Fills the sky,
A memorable moment,
Fills the minds,
Of nations so poor,
Yet more colours unfold,
And children do yield,
To passions unknown,
Forever to be shown,
In young people's minds.

Who will pass on,
Their true to mind thoughts,
In their destined future,
Which no one will see,
Until that day eventually arrives,
So for now,
Our young generation,
Of every nation,
Just soaks up this unexplained texture,
Of colours so wonderful.

Yet in a gasping moment,
The colours have faded,
So unexpectedly,
There's a feeling of sadness,
Now filling the empty air,
But peace stays within every heart and mind,
Like the memory of this solemn moment,
It'll stay within every mind.

Hannah Christine Victoria Metcalfe (17) Raines
Foundation School

School Dinners

Dinners, dinners every day
Sometimes hot
And sometimes cold
Smelly, sizzling sausages
Sizzling hot for us to eat
Hot as fire
And cold as ice
Dinners, dinners every day

There's so much on the menu
And a little to choose
Similar dinners every day
All cooked in the same way
Some are soggy
Some are sweet
Dinners ready for us to eat

Julia Khanom (13) Sarah Bonnell School

Cutting Trees

Cutting down trees
Why do people cut trees? I asked myself.
They chop trees down and produce
Carbon dioxide.
Why not stop? If it's bad
Soon all the ice block in Iceland will
melt and the Earth will be destroyed.
Why not stop? It it's bad, I asked again.
'Stop' while there's a chance
That's my advice.

Rimni Begum (14) Sarah Bonnell School

Don't See

Don't see my colour
Just see my face
We all belong to the human race

Don't see my colour
Don't see my creed
Why do you read me like a book

Don't stop and stare
But take a second look
Upon my bones not on my flesh.

Stop living life in black and
                    white.
Don't see no colour at all
We want to be equal we want to
                    be fair

So don't see my colour
Just see my face
We all belong to the human race

Cheryl Stevenson (13) Sarah Bonnell School

Shetland Disaster

Shetland disaster, a pollution disaster
Seals, spotted with coats of oil
Otters and thousands of sea birds
Are at risk as sticky, slick spreads
Slick of death, slick of doom
They are not bothering with fish
as there are too many
The Shetland coast is one of so
many

Shetland disaster, a timebomb disaster
fierce winds and rushing water
More and more oil spills out
Detergent is dropped
Still it does not matter
Everything has died away

The tanker sinks
Is this the end
Or is it just the beginning?

Belinda Sarfo (13) Sarah Bonnell School

Recycle Guard Rap

Listen up and listen hard
I'm gonna be your recycle
guard.
My name's Natasha and
I'm the best.
I recycle my paper and
all the rest.
So you do the same
and you'll be the best.
Remember recycle your
Paper *recycle* - paper and
        tins
        plastic
        and
        bottles
Keep this world a tidy place
Don't just chuck rubbish
on the floor.
Recycle Recycle

Natasha Walker (13) Sarah Bonnell School

Save Our Home

Save our home! Save our home!
Let us not destroy the world we live in.
Let us not destroy
God's work by polluting our home.

Save our home! Save our home!
Let us not destroy the world we live in.
Let clean oxygen be the only air.
Without poisonous fumes adding to it.

Save our home! Save our home!
Let us not destroy the world we live in
We must not let litter
Make our home a
Second-hand junkyard.

Save our home! Save our home!
Let us not destroy the world we live in.
We must put a stop to
this big problem of ours.

Let the next generation also
see the beauty of reality of Mother Nature.
and not just in picture books.

Save our home! Save our home!
Let us not destroy the world we live in
Let us all build up.
Our home and make it a better place to live in.

Save our home! Save our home!
Before it's too late.

Amina Ceesay (14) Sarah Bonnell School

Human Greed

The humans arrived,
With huge machines
To rip up the grassland,
Dotted with trees.

They looked up at the sky,
But it wasn't there.
There were beaks, talons,
And wings instead.

The beaks, talons and wings,
Of the hawks,
Who were ready to attack,
If the humans didn't go.

The humans were mesmerised.
Their brains told them to run,
But their feet remained on the ground,
And wouldn't even budge.

Each hawk chose a human,
Whom he could attack.
Then suddenly they ran,
But the hawks knew,
That they would be back.

Feeroza A S Patel (13) Sarah Bonnell School

Pocket Money

We want some pocket money!
We want some pocket money!
We won't eat our food 'til we get some pocket money!

We want some pocket money
To make our purses look muscular and bulky.
If we don't get pocket money
We'll act silly and sulky.

We want some pocket money
So we can go out at night
If we don't get pocket money
We'll go on strike.

Parent's are stingy
And don't give us enough.
If we don't get our pocket money
We'll start acting tough.

We'll wash the car
And cook the dinner
Oh *Please!*
Give us some pocket money.

That's it! That's it!
We're going on strike,
We won't go to school
And we won't do our homework.

We want some pocket money!
We want some pocket money!

Zaheera Y Munshi (13) Sarah Bonnell School

Pollution

Pollution is here
Pollution is there
Pollution is everywhere
with litter here
with a cloud of smog there
with dangerous gases in the air
Global warming
Must be stopped
before the world
begins to rot

Laurna Gooding (14) Sarah Bonnell School

The Whales

The whales on the coast,
Tumbling, turning on the ocean bed.
Full of joy and happiness,
As the sun meets the sea.

Happy as clowns in the ocean mist,
As their beautiful singing,
Meets the ears.
Corruptive boats approach the horizon,
The whales unaware of their fate.

I could hear them crying,
Screaming for my help.
A tear trickled down my face,
As a sea of red blood,
Washed up upon the shore.

As the poachers sailed away,
No sound was to be heard.
The red sea was lonely,
So quiet you could hear a pin drop,
No whales on the coast.

I will never forget,
The day the poachers came.
Now all we have are picture books and
                              shoe wax
to remind me of,
The beautiful blue whale.

Sarah-Anne Veal (13) Sarah Bonnell School

Pollution

I ask the people what pollution is;
I ask the people what destruction is;
I ask them who pollutes the world;
I ask them who destroys the world;
Is it me? or is it you?
'Tell me, tell me please will you.'
Pollution! Pollution!
'Well it's those rich people who own
factories and big fancy cars.' It's them, It's them
we say it is.
I ask the people what pollution is;
I ask the people what destruction is;
I ask them who pollutes the world;
I ask them who destroys the world;
Is it me? or is it you?
'Tell me, tell me please will you'
Destruction! Destruction!
'Well it's those rich people owning huge companies
mills and factories, they're the people who send men
to Brazil, New Zealand and many other countries to
cut down our precious Rain Forest, and destroy other
pieces of land.'
We told you it's rich people didn't we.
I ask the people what pollution is;
I ask the people what destruction is;
I ask them who pollutes the world;
I ask them who destroys the world;
Is it me? or is it you?
Tell me, tell me please will you . . .

Sumaiya Banu Chikhalia (14) Sarah Bonnell School

89

Pollution

Pollution, pollution, I wonder what it is?
People say it's the rubbish we throw away,
People say it's the oil that's in the sea,
People say it's CFC's,
But I wonder what it really is?

Pollution, pollution, I wonder what it is?
The rubbish is piled up like a mountain,
The sea is as black as the night sky,
Why aren't all sprays ozone friendly?
But I still don't know what pollution really is?

Pollution, pollution, I wonder what it is?
The ozone layer is breaking up,
Why can't people see?
People have different views on pollution,
But everyone is guilty,
Of throwing something away,
that could have been recycled,
But I still don't know what pollution is?

Tajinder Khunghara (12) Sarah Bonnell School

Litter

Litter, why litter?
Sometimes I wonder, why there's litter?
In Schools and in public places
People always make litter.

Litter, why litter?
Sometimes I wonder, why there's litter?
If there was no litter,
Our environment would be clean.

Litter, why litter?
Sometimes I wonder, why there's litter?
Litter is destroying our environment
Litter can even be dangerous.

Litter, why litter?
Sometimes I wonder why there's litter?
Someone asked me,
'Why can litter be dangerous?'
I answered back, 'broken bottle.'

Litter, why litter?
Sometimes I wonder, why there's litter?
Litter can be as sharp as a sword,
Litter can hurt and make others cry.

Litter, why litter?
Sometimes I wonder, why there's litter?

Aleya Begum (14) Sarah Bonnell School

Walking Home

As I was walking home.
On an autumn's day
I stepped on a pile of leaves.

They crunched, crackled and
crinkled.
And went all over the place.

The leaves are paper balls.
All crinkling and crackling.

The leaves were as red as blood.
Orange as the sun and
Yellow as cheese in
My mother's cupboard.

The colours shone in the sun.
Like the gold in my hand.

Runa Patel (12) Norbury Manor High School

The Sun

The sun was like a fireball
My lemonade was really cool.
The sand was burning all my toes
The tomato on my face was my sunburnt nose.

I ran to the sea and jumped straight in
It was then I remembered I couldn't swim
I flapped in the water like a fish on a hook
Still at least in the water I wouldn't cook.

Kate Pitt (12) Norbury Manor High School

Washing Accident

I trundled into the bathroom.
Turned on the basin taps,
Out came the water like a waterfall,
I fell asleep on the bathroom floor,
Splish, splash, bang, crash.
There's water dripping on me.

Help! Help! Help!
Help me someone please,
The water was a whirlpool,
Whooshing and swooshing,
Like a storm on a raging sea,
And there's no way of knowing,
There's water dripping on me.

It's flowing out of control.
Down the stairs and into the street.
Like a drum banging a beat,
Down the road faster and faster,
And the water was a river,
Still dripping on me.

Then drip, drip, drip,
Drip I awoke with a bang
Like a tambourine clang,
It seems to me that it was all a dream,
But wait, there's water dripping on me.

Kelly Price (12) Norbury Manor High School

My Friend Ria

My friend is a girl with bright blond beautiful hair.
She's always shouting, talking and dancing without a care,
With a head the shape of the world.
And once I saw her with her body all curled,
She cares about animals and has got twenty nine pets,
And is always going on about her great Aunt Bet.
She always talks about that tickling take that
And is always saying that Hairy Hiccuping Howard's far too fat.
I think you've guessed who I'm talking about now,
Yes it's Ria my friend, come take a bow.

Siobhan Marie Goddard (12) Norbury Manor High School

Sea Dreams

The music of the ocean lives in it's majestic glory.
I feel the silky fingers engulf me as my mask holds my world -
I used to swim through the cool waters of night,
As gentle starlight dappled the rippling surface.
I used to lie on my back, drinking in the cascading stars,
As the cool water held me up to life.

Can I dive down below the sunwarmed waters?
Down into the darkness and cold beyond.
I want to feel again the crushing pressure,
As my lungs burst, my eyes burn, and my ears sing.

I want to feel again the raw power of the sea as it takes me to its
heart -
And here I will lie for all eternity.
Bury me where the sun lights the waters by day and the benthos
lights the waters by night.
Commit my body to the sea so that my soul may forever roam the
oceans.

Sylvia Spence (18) Esher Sixth Form College

Freedom

Looking out of my prison bars,
I imagine I transform into a
        great bird.
My wings open wide causing the
        dust on the floor to swirl.
Then I fly out of my cruel cell.
I soar high into the blue, warm sky.
The Guardsmen shoot.
Their bullet's are no match for my strong
        and powerful wings.
As a bird I am free,
free to glide left and right
free to swoop up and down
free to do a I please.
The wind crashes coolly against my face.
I know that I am free.
As I dive down into the water I turn
        into a silver fish.
Flicking my tail as hard as I can,
        I look like a bullet darting
        through the water.
I jump out of the water only to
        splash straight back in and swim
        in circles.
Dizziness overtakes me and I head
        towards the bank and reform into
        a man.
Then slowly and cautiously I walk
        away to freedom.

Barry K Clarke (16) Gordons School

97

School Dinners

School dinners are really sick!
Cold as well you betta be quick,
Hot dinners are the very worst,
On the plate the sausages have burst,
On the table there's food squashed in,
Lots and lots of food dropped round the bin.

Dinner is nicer than the lunch,
I know no-one ever eats brunch,
Near the hall it smells quite foul,
Now the pastry tastes like a towel,
Everyone does not pay the bill,
Running home I'm writing my will.

Samantha Wright (13) Gordons School

The Hippopotamus

What is a hippo?
It is a grey heavy thing;
It has stumpy legs;
It has a short tail;
It is large.
It wallows in mud.
It eats all night.
It's definition of me;
I do all that;
Weight carried with it.

Jeffrey Foy (11) Gordons School

Life v Death

Life is on its last legs,
It's starting to lose speed
Death who was far behind,
Is catching up.
Life is running on adrenaline now,
Death gets fresher every pace,
Life can see the line, it gets there,
But collapses just before.
Death is running the final straight,
And life tries to drag itself across the line,
Death puts on an extra spurt of speed,
And crosses just before life.
Life gives up and dies.

Simon Henderson (16) Gordons School

Bottoms Up

My mummy crept up and washed me
I never had time to complain:
She was under my shawl.
With a cotton wool ball.
And by crikey she's done it again.

I was living in Wattery Splendour.
In a nappy so warm but wet.
When my mother came up and washed me.
And I haven't got over it yet.

Does a boy have no choice in the matter?
Can't a boy call his bottom his own?
No! She pulls down the sheet, gets hold of my feet.
And she won't leave my bottom alone.

Martin Murray (14) Gordons School

Wonderland

When I look at the sky,
I say, 'Oh why can't I fly,'
I look up above,
and I see a grey dove,
I turn back,
and look at the muddy track,
and I wonder why.

In times like these,
oh someone help me please,
I cannot even afford a shoe,
what can I do?
Is there anyone out there,
that has anything spare?
And now all that I have left is my keys.

Darren Jordan Pasley (14) Gordons School

A Dirty Pig

What is a dirty pig?
   A dirty pig is fat and bristly,
Its eyes twinkle in the mud,
   Its snout big and covered in food,
Its legs short and fat,
   Its tail as curly as a corkscrew,
Its nose as stumpy as a log.
         All in All
   He loves to play in mud!

Kimberly Walker (13) Gordons School

Growing Old

Growing old, many people
don't worry about their
age any more.

When bones are stiff,
hands refuse to be
gentle and kind,
don't give me your pity.

When I'm old and wrinkled
don't look at me if I'm a
fool, just treat me like
a human being for once.

Before you know what's
happened I would have
long past my sell by
date, so cheerio!

Thomas Straker (17) Gordons School

Horses

Horses are wonderful creatures,
Over the field they graze.
Riding is such fun,
So horses are so sweet and gentle,
Even if you do something wrong,
So I love horses because they're so sweet.

Louisa McGill (11) Gordons School

Being a Bird

I want to be free
so wonderful free
it is so nice to be free

I would like to be a bird
to fly in the air
to glide and to twit
to fly north and south
to be in the warmth
that's why I want to be free

Vicky Cliff (13) Gordons School

My Greenhouse

Bloody kids they're so annoying
each day they come plotting and ploying
I know their plans by gum I do
so I hide *My Greenhouse* with a boulder or two

They come to *My Greenhouse* and smash all the glass
but I'll beat 'em to it
and smash it myself
by gum I will

Smash!

William Fenton (15) Heathside School

The Fox and the Man

The car. The purring engine,
His foot almost hugging the
Pedal. Tiredness creeps around him like a
Burglar in his house.

He was going faster. Faster.
No one could catch him now.
His car an old Chevy, her
Speed and engine beginning to flow.

Out of the hedgerow. Spin the wheel.
Swerves, thought he missed it,
But he had with his heel.
A moment of silence then he hears a squeal.

He gets out, examines his victim
Still alive, but barely with him
His first thought, leave it on the road.
But he couldn't be that cruel.

The man loads the fox inside,
Hoping to find a vets open.
He feels the fox's pain.
Tiredness becomes an empty drain.

In the twilight, as rain falls,
The man and the fox,
Two of nature's tools.
Find a common ground in the Chevy tin box.

Jake Binnigton (14) Tiffin Boys School

Things at Night

Lying twitching in my bed,
Can't get those thoughts out of my head,
Slowly getting out, I need the loo,
But will the bogeyman jump out shouting 'boo'?
Running to the door, I'm nearly there,
But will he catch me on the stairs?
Quickly running past my brother's room,
I'm sure I saw him there in the gloom,
Now I'm at the toilet, it's nearly all out,
Imagining the bogeyman will jump out of it - the dirty lout,
Run to my room, slam the door
Sprint quickly across the floor
Jump in bed,
Pull the blankets over my head,
All I can hear is my breathing,
All I can hear is my heart beating,
Suddenly my bedroom door gives a creak,
I knew I shouldn't have gone for a leak,
Quickly I am armed with a table lamp,
I'll wham it over his head the dirty tramp,
Slam, I got him! Gosh aren't I bad?
Great Scot, oh Lord Almighty, I've just killed my Dad!

Chris White (13) Tiffin Boys School

Dreams

The lesson goes on,
Everyone dozing.
Dreams singing a song,
The learning is frozen.
Children all sleeping,
Falling away.
Falling till waketime,
Minds all a sway.
Then comes the bell,
Everyone wakes,
Then comes the smell
Of the canteen's own cakes.
The homework is given,
The smell brings on dozing.
To limbo we're driven,
Yet hunger awaking.

Peter J Bellamy (13) Tiffin Boys School

Night Poem

Night is the darkness
Night is the chill
Night is the death
It is there to kill

I look from my window
And what do I see
The owl is there
Glaring at me

On the grass, I stood
I was deep in the wood
I heard a sudden mooaan!
I was not alone

I'm in a deep sleep
Upon me the night creeps
Everything is silent
And I am asleep.

Michael Paul Gerrard (14) Tiffin Boys School

A Sleepless Night

As you fall into bed you're big trouble, and you've been thinking all
day.

Everything flashes through your mind, and you're really depressed.
You can't get to sleep, and you listen to the wind rustling up the
leaves,

And whipping through the trees cracking the branches on the
window.

Now you sit up, and there's an eerie silence downstairs,
And the stairs creak on the landing.
Now you turn the light on and you're sweating like mad.
Then the covers fly off in a heap on the floor.
You turn on the light, and read a book, but you still can't concentrate.
You take a gulp of water, and it goes straight to your
Bladder, next thing you know you're on the toilet.
You sit there thinking, roll on the morning!

Stephen Greatorex (13) Tiffin Boys School

My Nightmare

I sleep at night, full of dreams,
But one is as scary as ever,
Oh no! He's coming towards me,
What shall I do? Shall I run?
Many thoughts are roaming around my mind.
I know, I'll hide in that bin,
I sat there till I heard him walk past,
But I sneezed and I knew that was it.
I was so very scared and anxious,
Then suddenly he opened the lid,
He peered in and looked at me fiercely,
With his sharp long teeth staring over me,
He reached for me but then suddenly,
I woke up, relieved to see this dream fade away and die.

Matthew Hempel (14) Tiffin Boys School

Sleepless Night

Twisting, turning,
I can't sleep.
Clock ticking,
Tick . . . tick . . . tick.
I'll try counting sheep,
1 . . . 2 . . . 3 . . . 4,
11 . . . 12 . . . 13,
35 . . . 36 . . . 37,
Oh! It's no use.
Street lamp glares,
Through the curtains.
I look at my watch,
It says 2 o'clock.
I hear a car,
Closer, closer, and fades off,
Into the distance.
Tick . . . tick . . . tick,
For hours it seems.
The light outside gets brighter,
And so dawn breaks.

Siraj Yusuf (13) Tiffin Boys School

The Nightmare

As you lie back on your bed and close your eyes,
As darkness takes over the world.
Your muscles relax, and your body slows down,
As you move to a place untold.
Suddenly you're running up the steps,
The steps that are falling away.
You get nearer and nearer to the bottom step,
And will fall down if you stay.
You can't keep going so over you go,
Falling down through the empty space.
You want to stop but you can't you see,
So you put your hands over your face.
You are still falling, and falling so fast,
As if in a bottomless well.
You have fallen so far, so fast, so quick,
That you must be going to hell.
The glow of red comes nearer and nearer,
And the heat, and the must, and the smell.
You land in some ash, and it sprays everywhere,
And you're sure that this must be hell.
You turn around and see fear itself,
Fear of this red body with flame lace.
Those three red prongs with their points so sharp,
Just ready to run through your face.
The next moment you are awake,
With sweat dripping from your chest.
As you shiver with fear and are thankful for life,
You try not to think of the rest.

Matthew Turk (13) Tiffin Boys School

The Nightmare

I saw the video.
It was scary,
Killing, suspense, everything.
I went to bed not wanting to be alone.
In the dream I experienced a sensation.
One time light and beautiful colours.
Then dark, dark, dark, dark . . .
All that happened was dark and horrible things around me..
Then suddenly I was walking in paradise.
I knew at that moment I was in a virtual world.
Then I fell.
I fell for ages, upon ages, upon ages.
I saw things around me which should have been in my mind.
So soon as I saw everything,
I landed on a rubbish tip.
But immediately I heard an engine start.
It was a compactor!
Pushing from side to side and from top to bottom.
And when I was to be squashed,
I woke up.
Heart thumping,
Vivid of my nightmare.

Jason Chong (13) Tiffin Boys School

Alone

My parents go out, and I begin to groan,
All I can think of, is that I'm left alone.
The time is eleven, I begin to worry,
When they come home, they'll be sorry,
At seeing me dead, on my blood covered bed.
I begin to think of the ways I'll die,
Shot in the head? or stabbed through the eye?
All of a sudden, I hear a bump,
As fast as lightning, does my heart pump.
I dive under my bedcovers, waiting for the time,
That some cannibal will find me, and have a good dine.
All at once my face is without cover,
I flick my eyes open, and see the face of my kind, gentle mother.
With a sigh of relief, I dive to my mum,
So extremely pleased with my ordeal done.
My eyes glance at the clock,
My ears hear, there is no 'tick-tock'.
On its face it shows eleven,
I ask my mum for the time,
She says it's seven.
All of this worry was for nothing at all,
Now I feel nothing, but *very, very* small!

Alex Donaldson (14) Tiffin Boys School

The PSE Lesson

Be quiet! please class,
Line up in single file,
Eh?
Single file muffs!
Oh . . .
Briggs,
Yes Miss?
What are *you* doing?
Nothing Miss,
Well don't do it again then OK?
OK Miss,
Sit down class,
Sit down!
Yes Miss,
Now today we will talk about the *litter* problems,
Ow!
Who threw that?
. . . Nobody?
OK then *Litter Duty* at lunch time!
Groan!
Well that's solved let's change the subject,
Er?
OK let's talk about . . .
Clang clang clang,
Fire?
Fire alarm! Yippeeee!
Smoke!
That's solved the problem of school!

Peter Lewis (13) Tiffin Boys School

Dreaming

I lie in bed,
Waiting for sleep to overtake me.
The hoot of an owl from my window,
Startles me,
As it breaks the silence.
The moonlight casts an eerie shadow on my head,
A white light,
Fading, fading,
Until it's gone behind a cloud.
A faint gust of wind,
Rustles and swirls the thin layer of leaves on the path.
Now I'm falling down into oblivion,
Dreaming . . .
I'm in a tunnel,
A tiny spot of light at the end.
Racing forwards,
Towards the light,
But then,
The scene transforms beneath my eyes.
A clown,
A tent,
The circus.
Then a ringing,
Shrill and loud,
My alarm.

Michael Moreland (13) Tiffin Boys School

The Darkness of the Night

Through the mist of the night,
Was a strange eerie fright,
The owls were all hooting,
Calling for light.
Down in the darkness,
The animals lay,
Foxes and badgers,
Awaiting their prey.
The whistling wind,
Blew through the dead trees,
Arousing small creatures,
From the ground leaves.
Up in the sky,
The clouds were just drifting,
Birds in their nests,
Their heads only lifting.
Dawn then approaches,
Light had arrived,
Animals waking,
Their sleep is deprived.

Alexander Rothwell (13) Tiffin Boys School

Nightmares

I wake to howling heavy sounds,
Mice, cats, owls and hounds.
Guns booming in the air,
People yelling everywhere.
Cars with gangsters at the wheel,
Soldiers out for the kill.
Thugs rioting everywhere,
Smashing things here and there.
The old are scared and full of worry,
Running home in a hurry.
But wait and listen, loud above all,
I can hear a distinctive call
My mother is talking, full of care,
'Liam, it's only a *Nightmare!*'

Liam Thomas Parmenter (13) Tiffin Boys School

The Sleepless Night

A night of endless nothingness,
Lying there, with the seconds having seemingly stopped,
Shivering, in the almost black silence,
The howling wind the only sound the only movement,
I longingly wait for the dawning light,
The morning birds, and the alarm clock to break the silence
Those distant thoughts remain motionless.
The ticking clock becomes familiar,
As its ever present sounds continue on through the night,
My eyelids become heavier but I remain as alert as an eagle after its
                                                                    prey,

In bed, but sleep seems a distant priority,
I tussle with the duvet, perhaps taking my ever-increasing frustration
                                                                    out on it,

But still the seconds hardly move,
Staring at the clock, I think of the day head,
And fear my sleep catching, and taking its toll on me.
The morning cockerel crows and I realise my misery will soon
                                                                    decline,

The seconds, the minutes and the hours all become history,
As the morning light floods through the curtains,
Animals, birds and the morning cars all begin the day,
The new day is at last upon us.

Ben Tompkins (14) Tiffin Boys School

The Class Room

Children waiting for their teacher
outside the old, crumbly class room,
Paint peels from the walls and cobwebs hang down from the ceiling.
Hearing the echoing of her shoes clip clop down the corridor
they quickly form an orderly queue.

She stands so tall, way up high
and towers over the children like an eagle to its prey.
The repeats the usual phrase 'English, here we come' then in we
troop.
No one daring to speak a word or she'll pounce and bellow
Detention in your ear.
This goes on for the whole lesson
and nobody can wait till it's over!

Nicola Chalkley (14) George Abbot School

The Riding Lesson

I am so nervous today
I am having my first riding lesson
I have been told they can buck
And also reer up

Oh, I am so nervous today
I have been told they can bolt off and away
What happens if that's true
Just imagine what they'll do

I'm still nervous today
Oh look at the time
I have only an hour left
And I keep drinking lemon and lime

Mum I feel sick I feel sick
And I need the loo quick
Will it be big or small
Oh I really don't know

I'm now in the car
And we haven't got that far
But when we do arrive there
I hope my nervousness will go

Jacqueline Locke (13) George Abbot School

The Hunt

The doe ran for its life through the thick mountain woodland,
The hunting dogs were like machines: They wouldn't stop unless
they were shut down.
The men ran with their hunting rifles close behind.
The dogs closed in for the kill.
One snap.
The doe screamed in pain as blood started to flow from the wound in
her rear left leg.
Towards the cliff edge she ran.
A shot rang out and a bullet whizzed past her head.
The dogs growled right behind her.
Another snap.
Another scream of pain.
Along the cliff she ran.
A jump of a dog and it was on her back.
Teeth jabbed into her flesh.
Then, turning towards the cliff edge, without a hope in the world,
without thinking . . .
A leap into the unknown.

James Roc (13) George Abbot School

125

Mister Frog

Sitting on a log,
Swimming in the pond,
Hopping round a bog,
What a life to lead!

No school work to do,
No worries, at all,
No school dinners too,
What a life to lead!

Luck, lucky frog,
Do you know what I'd give,
To sit on a log,
Every day, all the time
Lucky, lucky frog!

Sarah Louise Jarrett (14) George Abbot School

My First True Romance

Blue eyes, blonde hair,
      sweet smile, good looks.
A boy so handsome,
      And very kind too.

I met him at the disco,
      He asked me to dance.
We found we really liked each other,
      And that was just a start.

We go the cinema,
      The park as well.
We sometimes go shopping,
      Or go into town.

We go places together,
      Almost every weekend.
Even sometimes on a school day,
      When we help each other work.

I'm mad about him,
      He's crazy about me.
We both love each other,
      My first true romance.

Nicola Exell (12) George Abbot School

Man

Man! What a creature
Enormous in battle
Tiny when cowering
I, for one, detest man
Even though I am one
I fear man
Even though I am one
I try to shut out man
Even though I am one
But what about man
Why does man hate itself
So much that it destroys itself
There are so many reasons
They can come up with
But their excuses are feeble
I, for one, detest man
Man! What a creature

Paul Cruickshank (13) George Abbot School

Panda

Panda alone in his cage people shouting at him and laughing at him when he did something like play with a tyre or chew on a bamboo stick.

They got him a lady friend so he would mate, they think he is a toy who likes to be stared at all day long.

There are hardly any Panda's around, maybe if they were left in the wild there might be more in this world.

Joanne Lilly (14) George Abbot School

The Childhood Dream

The childhood dream comes and goes,
and parents say no, no, no!
Children say please mummy please,
and all they say is well I'll see.

A Pilot, an Acrobat or maybe,
even a clown with a hat.
Every child has to be
something they like funnily.

Every dream is supernatural
for every child has to have
a dream of what they're
going to be.

If any child wants to sing,
or be a writer like Paul Jennings,
it's up to them.

Lindsey Magill (13) George Abbot School

If I Had a Great Big Hamburger

If I had a great big hamburger
I'd munch it all day long
I'd have some for my breakfast
For lunch and tea

If I had a great big hamburger
It would last the whole year through
I'd have an extra bit on my birthday
And save some for Christmas tea

If I had a great big hamburger
I'd have lots of ketchup
Some cheese
And maybe some lettuce too

If I had a great big hamburger
I'd give some to my friends
And maybe my brother too
But I'd leave the rest for me

If I had a great big hamburger
I'd take it everywhere with me
I'd take it on holiday
And to school with me

If my great big hamburger
Had all gone
I'd nip down to the local shops
And buy another one

Matthew Outterside (12) George Abbot School

131

The Unforgivable Sin

When you're young it's unforgivable sin,
To be who you really are,
To break loose from the metal jaws,
That hold you in a false dramatic pose,
Crippling inside you the lost child of yesterday . . .

The child who acted without inhibition,
Whose self-consciousness and vanity were as weak as a
unicellular being,
And to whom nerves were an undiscovered species.

But that child is a teenager now,
With self-consciousness as strong as an army of thousands,
And he laughs at the 'clueless' middle-aged man,
Labelled 'clueless' merely because he has freed his lost child,
And lives as his true self not some image crazed zombie,
Lost in utopia fantasy.

But perhaps if that child could for one moment,
Break free from the metal jaws of peer group pressure,
And show that teenager who he really is,
He could set him free,
And let him commit *The Unforgivable Sin.*

Bob Barbour (13) George Abbot School

The Homeless Girl

She's as free as a dove,
Flying alone,
No-one to answer to,
Left in the wilderness,
Facing the world,
With its day to day perils,
With nowhere to run to,
No shoulder to cry on,
For she is homeless,
Just one of the crowd.

Verity Anne Buchanan (13) George Abbot School

She Feels No Different

In all other ways
She is the same as you or I,
She feels no different
Yet,
She has never observed the world around her,
She cannot begin to imagine what colour must be like
And
She recognises objects only by their shape, smell or sound.
She does not see the strange fear in other's eyes as they look at
Her.
She is the same as you or I,
She feels no different
But,
She is robbed of her sight,
She is blind.

Helen Milbourn (13) George Abbot School

The Polar Bear

His pure white shiny fleece,
Drips wet after his dive,
He hauls himself from the hole,
With a roar of exhilaration.

He wanders across the snow covered plain,
A white smudge on the vast white wilderness,
He strives across the open ground,
To yet another feeding place,

With a tremendous leap and dive he
submerges,
Through the icy waters he goes,
A graceful beast once more,
Suddenly he sights his quarry.

Through the waters he glides like a bird in
the sky,
The seals panic and soon split up,
With his skilful eye he singles one out,
Towards this one he effortlessly slides,

With a thrust of his powerful paw,
And a snap of his gaping jaw,
The seal hangs limply between his teeth,
This is the life of the great white bear.

Matthew Brooking (13) George Abbot School

Tiger Tiger

Tiger, tiger as you peer through the bars of
your cage,
What goes through your mind?
You pace up and down your prison,
Watching, waiting, stopping, starting,
Anxious and troubled,
What must you be thinking?

As you look out at the crowd, with your
hypnotising eyes,
Staring beyond the people,
What must you be sensing?

The trees, the woods, the fields beyond,
Away from the bustle of the city.
Is that where you want to be,
Thinking, sensing, happy?

Craig Champness (13) George Abbot School

The Perfect Goodbye

Today was the day I'd been dreading to come.
I woke up to brilliant sunshine, outside! but it was
raining in my heart.
I wouldn't see him again for six whole months.

Slowly I got out of bed and washed. I got into the
dress I was wearing the day we met.
Such happy days, going for walks along the beach,
Staying in by the fireside.

I walked to his house, we would drive from there.
He said here is your present. He handed me a box
with holes in. Before you open it, I want you to
promise to name it after me. Oh! it was a puppy.
      I'll name it Sam.
      That's your name.

Philippa Louise Carmichael (13) George Abbot School

The Subway

Hustle, Bustle,
Push and shove,
An old orange here,
An apple core there.
Skippity, hoppity,
Children play.
Jumping, pouncing,
A cat and a mouse.
Then from afar,
A little child screams.
It echoes around,
So piercing and harsh.
Hustle, bustle
Push and shove,
This is a subway's life.

Clare Harrison (13) George Abbot School

Closed for Good!

Today was the day.
The book shop closed for good.
Boxes were piled high to the ceiling,
Packed to the brim with different books.

Eventually the lorry came,
A big burly man began to take all the boxes out.
He took them right pass me,
There went Catherine Cookson.

Then the Teen books went past,
That was it, I couldn't watch.
I ran quickly out of the back door.
When I went back the books were gone.

The big man had now started on the window.
He started to nail boards across them.
I began to cry, tears streamed down my face.
I couldn't believe it was happening.

Then the lorry was gone,
Chugging down the street.
That lorry had all that was dear to me in it.
That was it the book shop was closed for good!

Anna Gifford (13) George Abbot School

I Sit Beside the Fire and Think

I long for scenes where man has never trod,
A place where woman has not laughed or wept,
At one with my creator God,
And here I sleep, as I, in childhood sweetly slept.

In peaceful surroundings I lie,
Undisturbed by love or hate,
Under the beauty of God's blue sky,
No worries of death, or future fate.

Too hot the eye of heaven shines,
So as I drowsily wake from dreams forgot,
I think of love, life, of death,
And I wonder; why do humans not know when to stop?

                And, maybe I cry.

But alas, I in the scene am all alone,
A companion, please God,
A friend to share with me,
The scene where man has never trod.

                But, is this what I really want?

Ian Allardyce (13) Glyn School

My First Day at School

People everywhere, running jostling for space,
Suddenly a piercing sound, the whistle blows.
Children line up like soldiers,
On the vast grey blanket - play stops, Silence!

My first day - like a frightened cat,
Shivers, running down my spine.
My mother's hand gives comfort -
Like a bird in a warm cosy nest.

We go inside the big black building,
Not knowing what lies ahead.
Tables cluttering up the classroom,
Like houses on an estate.

I survey the enormous room,
Still clutching my new school bag,
She smiles, her eyes twinkling like raindrops.
My fear subsides, perhaps it won't be bad!

Oliver Dodd (13) Glyn School

Stormy Thoughts

I sit imprisoned in my house
Listening to the thunder cracking.

The rain pours down filling the gutters
My door creeks with the wind once again.

Filling my thoughts with bitterness,
I sit alone in the darkness.

I feel as if entombed in the cold
With bitter wind rushing around the forest outside.

Then the thunder strikes again and again
The rain outside beats

Against the misty countryside,
Splashing in the ponds,

Lashing in the woods.
the door swings open,

The icy wind rushes in
Making my legs go numb,

Then my arm
I am unable to move.

My blood freezes
And my heart stops,

Chains imprison me
I am now left alone forever with my stormy thoughts.

Chris Muscutt (13) Glyn School

Cyril the Centipede

Cyril the centipede
Loved playing games,
And his favourite one was baseball.
But when he played bowl
With nine fleas and a mole
Nothing could rouse his concentration.
They played spiders and newts
But his hundred boots
Gave his team very little to do
And the fleas would get bored,
For they just couldn't score
And the crowd would just stand there and boo!
'till one awful day, the crowd stayed away,
And no fans from either side came,
But all said and done
When it's none, none, none, none,
It's really not much of a game!

Carlos Dunn (13) Glyn School

Food Food Food

Don't give me any more curry, mum,
Nor stuffing or cauliflower cheese,
They have an awful effect on my poor tum,
And I don't get to sleep till three am for many weeks
      to come,
But I know you're only trying to please.
Your Chinese stir fry - now that is good,
And your mandarin cream pie,
As a special treat your steak and kidney pud
Now, for that I would die.

My favourite dish of them all is chicken pasta bake
With chunks of chicken and loads of melted cheese.
Followed by a nice big bowl of wobbly jelly!
But a close second is a nice thick juicy steak
Accompanied by French fries, mushrooms and peas.
So, please mum, remember no more rotten food that
      gives me Delhi belly.

John Malyon (13) Glyn School

The Mariner's Log

Our boat is bleached by streams of light
Our throats are dry, our lips are tight
Our mouths are parched in scorching heat
But life goes on, however bleak.

Still not a sign of wind upon the sea
The torture goes on in agony
Our spirits break down, our heads are low
It seems as if there is no place to go.

The air is still, the heat gets worse
We suffer beneath the sea bird's curse.

Onur Gilleard (13) Glyn School

Imagination

My mind is full of muddled thoughts,
It's difficult to say.
What is this, What is that,
like sorting the post everyday.

Imagination's a wonderful thing,
Nothing bars it's aim.
It's allowed to roll on endlessly,
like the sea's waving game.

Bits of this, Bits of that,
In my mind this day.
Like a Scouter's Jumble Sale,
Selling things for the pay.

Michael Blakeburn Glyn School

People

People bustle to and fro
Where they go nobody knows
People will sometimes stop and stare
Often than most they won't even care
People will get on with their lives
Go home to their parents, husbands and wives
Occasionally they'll stop and sit and think
Of what's in the oven, the kitchen sink
And people blame others for their petty mistakes
Start, stop relationships whilst broken hearts ache
People have ruled, worked and died
People have murdered, argued and cried
People will love, mate, give birth
Bring new life to an industrialised earth
People paint toes and talk on phones
Pray to God and worship stones
People will invade others' lands
People will lend a helping hand
People will meet and make good friends
People go on till the world ends

Simon Swift (16) Glyn School

No Limits

Dark days,
Angry hours,
Deep resentment
For the leader.
So he sat upon a cliff edge
Pondering in his heart,
What had happened to his life.

He was alright,
Had good friends
Until the day
That bloke came.

His name was Richard
He was a fascist.
White as white could be.
All of a sudden
Friends disappeared
And reappeared
Friends no more
In Richard's 'gang'
And he was left alone
To suffer the consequences.

His only sin
Being black
But that was sin enough.

They pushed him around
Stole his bag,
And threw all its contents
Across the field.
All through Richard's orders.

And so he fell
To the waves
Which engulfed him
With a meagre splash.
And no struggle from his body,
As he sank,
Sank downwards
Towards freedom
From his colour.

Michael Darke (15) Glyn School

The Death of the Soldier

There he lay death daunting him,
With pain as sharp as knives,
He heard the strident cries of pain,
From soldiers losing lives.

Slowly his life started to fade,
Like the wax of a candle melting away,
He knew it would not be long now,
For, this is the place he would stay.

For him darkness would be forever,
Life would be a dream,
And as the new day dawned,
His breath ebbed away like a stream.

Shaun Bennett (14) Glyn School

The Wind

A little boy called Robert Rose,
Whenever blowing or wiping his nose,
Would often make a pose.
Sometimes he would stretch his arm out,
Or sometimes give himself a clout.

One day when Robert was making a pose,
The wind happened to blow,
And there was Robert, on his toes,
While all his friends shouted *Yo!*

There was Robert thinking of anything,
When something in his brain went *Ping!*
'I'll just wait till the wind blows,
Then I'll show my friends what I know!'

Unfortunately for Robert Rose the wind never blew,
So that will show all you boys and girls what the wind can do.

Previn Jagutpal (13) Glyn School

Parody of the Ancient Mariner

It is a cruel headmaster,
And he stoppeth one of three.
'By thy sharp moustache, and glassy
eye,
Now wherefore stopp'st that me?'

The classroom doors are opened wide,
The register is called.
I must be in before the bell
You cannot keep me stalled.

He held him with his beady eye,
'I'm Deputy Head,' said he,
'And boys will do what I say,'
He whispered evilly.

This man had an obsession,
To patrol around the school,
To catch unruly schoolboys,
Who have disobeyed the rules.

Chris O'Doherty (14) Glyn School

The Ancient Cricketer

It is an ancient cricketer and he
stoppeth one of three,
'By thy grass stained whites and
wooden bat,
Now wherefore stoppeth me?'

He held him with his cricket glove,
And the young man stood still,
And listens like a three year's child,
The cricketer hath his will

'The many batsmen so skilful and they
all '*out!*' did lie,
And a thousand, thousand spectators
watched disgusted and so did I

Alone, alone, all all alone,
Alone I batted till tea
And Christ would not take pity on
my arms in agony.

The silly clouds above the pitch,
That so long remained,
I dreamt they were full of dew,
And later that minute it rained.

Water, water everywhere
Poured down from clouds so grey
Water, water everywhere,
Rain at last stopped play!

Philip J Christie (13) Glyn School

153

Anger

I'm so mad I could scream

I stormed upstairs,
Crying as I went,
Stopping only at the top to say,
'You don't care anyway.
I was red in the face from screaming
and shouting.
I ran to my room
Lay down on my bed
And said 'You wouldn't care if I was dead.'
I ranted and raged
Nearly twice a day
But this was the worst
Everyone would say.
And all of it over just one little fight.
I felt like exploding,
Stamping my feet,
I didn't though,
The floorboards were weak.
I hated my brother
He always won in some way or another.
I felt like hitting him
Making him dead,
But after a while
After some thought,
I said, 'no I know what I'll do,
I'll make friends
Yes that's what I'll do.'

Megan Lewis (15) Salesian School

A Warm Summer's Evening

The sun sinking slowly, setting silently;
Buzzing bees flitting from plant to plant,
Collecting pollen as they go.
A gentle breeze, as soft as feathers,
Blowing summer scents subtly towards the old house.
Finally, all is dark, casting shadows,
Like reflections in a pool

Nicola Eaves (12) Salesian School

In a World full of Televisions . . .

I see . . .
A bookshelf full of books of thought,
Mirrors making images of what has been,
Figures fighting in neighbours,
Visions in my mind whizzing like a whirlpool,
Cowboys' guns shooting in victory in a war,

I see . . .
Sorrow and unhappiness, sobbing, crying,
People's blank faces in a black n' white film,
Silver mist with people calling for someone lost,
Figures surfing on a hot, sandy beach,
Waves crashing down,
                    down,
                            down
                                on my visions.

Jennifer Reynolds (11) Tolworth Girl's School

The Boat Trip

A
boat
floats on
the stream,
It can be blue,
black or even
green. The waves
push the boat into the sea, it swirls
around as happy as can be. The wind
forces the sail to go, it rushes to the
river and it starts to flow

Anujah Srinivasan (11) Tolworth Girl's School

Green

Gorgeous green glimmers in the
light.
Like cucumbers crisp, clean and bright,
Grass in the summer with flowers in
between.
But what would be greener than green.

Kelly Hepple (12) Tolworth Girl's School

Writing a Poem

I'm sitting here writing this poem
And I really don't know what to write.
I'd better think of something quick,
Or I'll be here all night.

I'll have to come up with a brainwave,
Some very clever idea,
But I'm not going to think of anything
And that's crystal clear.

Elaine J Round (11) Tolworth Girl's School

The First Nativity

The angels all wore tinsel,
that sparkled in the light.
One shepherd brought a
sheepskin rug,
to keep him warm at night,
no-one wet their knickers
and everything was fine,
'till a wise man clearly stated
'I bring you Frankenstein!'

Kate Gallon (12) Tolworth Girl's School

Problems

Problems come and problems go,
But they'll all be solved, you should
know,
If you think about them well,
They won't make life as bad as hell.

Problems come from here and there,
But you'll soon find out that most
are fair,
If you solve them well enough,
They won't make life too tough.

Problems come and make you think,
When they're solved you'll be tickled pink,
More will come but it's not that bad,
So there is no reason to be sad.

Sadeem Alsaid (14) Beverley School

Innocence

Youth in his arms,
Held up by hands,
Worn and bony,
The lines of knowledge,
Experience,
Show on his face.
the child's smooth, soft skin,
Innocent
Of the harshness of life.
Experience smiles at the joy
Of his young grandchild.
Carefree,
All in rags,
On his shoulders,
He sees only the sun,
Only the flying insects,
Buzzing past,
And does not see the harsh
Bare ground.

Beatrice Holford (15) Broadwater School

Together

Walking happily down the dusty road,
The light sides of their faces
Contrasting with the dark.
Grandpa's old, worn face
Holds glistening eyes, laughing happily,
Catching the blue sky,
Striking out, touching me.
Next to his,
A clear, childish face,
Soaking up his experience.
The worked, leathered hands
Protect,
Holding the small body with ease.
Joining as one,
The young and old
Sharing something special.
Their feelings for each other
Reflecting in their dark eyes.

Chantelle Marshall (15) Broadwater School

Protection and Safety

The boy clings tightly,
around the safe, strong, protective shoulders
of experience.
The father holds his boy lightly.
Nothing will touch his pride
and joy of this world.
His brave face belies his worker's hands.
The child bemused, puzzled,
confused,
so many sights and sounds.
His eyes show flecks of fear
against the bleakness that surrounds.
He stands
whilst his father crouches,
holding him.
A picture of trust
formed from love in the face of adversity.

Matthew Poole (16) Broadwater School

Memories

During the blazing hot summer days when the sun was high
Granddad and I would journey down to the fruit bearing fields
And pick the blood red, sweet tasting fruits.
It used to be
One for me
One for my can -
When we had killed our cravings we trudged unhappily through the
pasture
Leaving the undisturbed creation behind.
Over the palisade and into the back porch,
Where Nan was expecting us,
Spoon in hand,
To make sugary jam
To spread on my bread.

It broke my heart to see the fruit's dying
Covered in a marl-grey blanket, and being the feast
Of a soft brown blob of a creature
Trailing its silvery slime.
When the time came
For the season to cease
I knew, I would still relish the year to come.

Rachel Fuller (15) Broadwater School

Young Child

A young child scared,
Holding on to security
In the dark, dull atmosphere.
Her tiny hands enclosed
Around a tree trunk leg,
Protecting her from an unknown danger.
The girl's eyes reflecting a fear,
Wanting to be comforted
The worry on her small face,
Expressing horror and fright.
But an older and wiser person
Stands to prevent evil from touching the child,
To show guidance and knowledge
Through the paths of life.
Making the directions clear
And the journeys steady.
Taking the right decisions
For peaceful moments in time.
the child is safe.
Safe in the hands of an adult.
The hands of warmth and care.

Linda Hirons (15) Broadwater School

Axl Rose

Long golden locks of hair cascades down his back
Eyes like whirlpools
Hypnotising, sea green
A voice like no other

His evil childhood blacked out
Severe hatred for himself
Violent moods
Mind separated from feelings
Crazy, psycho.

Lisa Wilde (13) Broadwater School

The Harpy

She stands on her taloned feet,
Ready for the next man thing to come,
She waits, her feathered breasts still,
Though her breath ragged.

The waiting ends, a man-thing comes,
And walks under her tree.
She launches herself toward the ground,
Tearing flesh and feather as she goes,
The man looks up in fright.

She stretches her feathered legs,
To tear him with her cruel feet,
he bats her away,
With a bag soggy with blood.
He feels in fear, for now she recognises him,
Perseus, the slayer of Medusa.

She turns to flee and fly,
But hears the sound of bone on sackcloth,
She turns and looks.
And falls to the ground.

Cold . . . stone cold.

James M Collett (13) Broadwater School

Cry of the Whales

'Mother what will become of me,
What will be my fate?
Will I live to see another day,
Or be murdered by greed or hate?'

'I cannot tell my precious son
But whilst you're by my side
Swift and graceful, smooth and gentle
Through the seas you'll glide'

Barbarians hunt us for our meat
They shoot and aim at me,
Vicious harpoons tear through our flesh
But 'there's more than one whale in the sea!'

'Mother who are our enemies
Who would do such a thing?'
Money and man are our enemies,
Lipstick and make-up they sing.

Amber C Lane (13) Broadwater School

169

Dolphin's Joy

Cascading across the sea as a blanket of blue satin holds
Back and looks inside her innermost fears.
Her elegant and graceful moves
Seem unnatural for such a large creature.

Rotating in a world of cruelty
The harp sound of a dolphin's
Cry echoes into the sunset
Carrying memories of those she loved.

Nicola Rodger (13) Broadwater School

Creature

Sitting on the deadly trap that is her home,
The creature rears her ugly head.
Senses the vibrations of the poor soul,
Who is to be the next meal.

Scuttling nervously to the entrance of her dusty cavern,
She looks out on the 'giants',
Who, should they see her, would run in fear.

She pounces on an intruder,
Tangled in the bed,
Which only she may sleep in.

Wrapped in a silken death shroud,
All the victim feels is numb.
Then the sinking fangs and blackness,
Knowing its short life is over.

Replenished now,
The creature lifts all eight legs.
Then quickly, smoothly scampers toward daylight,
Feeling braver now.

the spider spins a sticky glazed web,
In a dark nook as the blood-red eyes rove the room.

Katie Marie Young (13) Broadwater School

Sheep

In a gently sloping field, the sheep are munching grass.
Totally oblivious as the cars go rushing past.
Till suddenly emerging from the mist of early morning
A fire engine is speeding, wailing, flashing, roaring.
The sheep are rudely wakened from their passive breakfast feast.
An awful interruption to serenity and peace.
They panic as a body, don't quite know where to go.
A blob of worried wool is rushing to and fro.
But soon the panic's over, the engines gone from view.
The sheep get back to munching grass, there's nothing else to do.

Susan Lake (13) Broadwater School

Old

She lives alone in her solitary house,
With no-one to talk to but the wind.
The bare interior of her home is only filled,
By a massive melee of mangled wool,
Destined to become a scarf
For her life is sadness and loneliness in truth
She can no longer hear the noise she once knew.
Not that there is a fraction of a sound to be heard in this deathly silence.
She lives to see tomorrow with no more purpose than that.

Julian Clift (13) Broadwater School

The Wood Hunter

Long, supple limbs pound the dry woodland floor,
Thudding through the crisp air.
Like well-oiled pistons, the lurcher's legs pump fear
Into the hearts of wood vermin.
Flashes of grey hair dart across the mighty oaks.

The lurcher comes to an abrupt halt, her ears
Prick, her eyes widen, she can see and hear her prey.
A squirrel!
The lurcher approaches, noiselessly, stealthily, she knows
The animal is hers.
The great dog breaks into a swift, crouching run,
Eyes fixed, the blood rushing in her ears.

The squirrel hears, and turns, only to look into
The eyes of death.
The lurcher pounces, jaws snapping viciously.
It is a clean kill, the squirrel dies instantly.
The lurcher picks up her prize, and trots away,
Tail erect.
She is the Queen of wood hunters, and she knows it.

Tom Dearsley (13) Broadwater School

Golden Lemur

His head stays motionless in the brilliant morning light.
His gleaming eyes glisten in the shimmers of the beautiful sunrise.
With the flickers that manage to penetrate the forest canopy of
mahogany teak and gum
He is poised ready to launch himself onto the neighbouring branches.
He sits perched in a potent position, pondering while studying the
bustling forest carpet.

The knowledge possessed in that miniature head seems to escalate
with time.
The soaring trees weave tantalisingly with his tortuous tail,
But this exemplary creature always has five fingers securely
anchored to the bough.

Alex Meade (12) Broadwater School

Turtle

Slowly ancient and deliberate -
The reputation of this fearsome beast!
His wizened years exact respect,
Withered limbs reveal his frailty,
But his eyes!
His eyes
Withhold naught
They disclose his true, loathsome self,
His descendance from the serpents of old
Plagued with a shell
He bides his time
To smile a blow
Against the inheritors of the earth
His ancestors were the masters of destruction
Of gargantuan proportions
But he -
Cursed with puny stature -
His eyes know all
His eyes shall destroy all!

Richard Harvie (15) Broadwater School

Travelling Home

Travelling home,
Sun beating down,
Creating strong, harsh shadows,
A youth holds an old, wooden cart,
His hands steadily gripping the long, thick handles.
He carries his brother, an alert child,
Cautious and stern-faced,
Not innocent, but experienced,
Hands placed firmly at the edge of the cart,
On the lookout.
Foliage litters the dusty track
Where the old and worn sandals tread,
Parallel to the barbed boundary.

Alex Sawyer (15) Broadwater School

Child

Buried in the protective clutch,
The naive child
Sits engulfed by security.
The man's decrepit, tired face
Showing affection and love
Towards the inexperienced bird
Nesting in his lap.
Her penetrating, brown eyes
Collecting the sun's gleam,
Her shiny visage
Benign,
Displaying innocence.
The dynamic, bright colours of youth
Contrasting with those naturally prosaic.

Marie Adlam (15) Broadwater School

Creature

Venturing through the jungle of
Life,
Guided by an experienced elder,
Pondering the branches of choice,
Hesitating at the veins of
Chance,
Regrets hanging over them,
Tempted by the green monster
Of envy,
They resist,
Continuing to travel the leaves
Of existence.

John Richard Draysey (15) Broadwater School

Squirrel

Leaping from tree to tree,
Taking no notice of me,
He stops,
He stares,
With his large eyes he glares,
At the evening sun through oak tree leaves,
His back is an arch,
As he sits upon the jagged branch, turning round,
He jumps to a nearby tree,
Scuttering home. He is free!

Helen Jackson (13) Broadwater School

A Hare

Earth-grey, and crouched in its own warmth,
A statuette, carved out of dew,
Its tapering ears catch the earthbound whispers
Of the trees in the early mind.
Taking the silent earth's pulse;
It quivers as a drawn bow,
In the watery wash of the sky.
The sun spills over the brim of the hill,
And, with a wild fey magic,
It is submerged in the flooding shadows
Which flee the light.
A glint of sunlit fur,
Hangs on the empty wind.

Harriet Earis (13) Broadwater School

The Wolf

Out from the mist
He runs
Out from the mist
He comes
The wind cold on his muzzle
Hungry for meat
Through forests
Through fields
He spies his prey
And takes the fallen lamb
The mist clears
And like the lightning
He is gone.

Simon Berry (14) Broadwater School

The Boy

The silence fills the air,
And his mysterious aura radiates outwards.
Naturally attractive and warm.
His eyes stare upwards.
Full of moody thoughts.
With a frown to accompany them.
Sitting draped across a chair.
Nothing mattering but his mysterious thoughts.
Dreams the images flickering across his face.
As the silence continues.

Katie Meade (14) Broadwater School

Racing the Tide

She races on,
Sleek and graceful,
Rhythm steady and regular,
Muscles rippling.
Coat a shiny mass of chestnut,
Hooves driving a beat on the sand.
She races on,
Competing against the raging wind,
And thundering through fuming waves,
Tailing streaming in all directions,
Mane tousled by the sea air,
Lashing out behind her.
She races on,
Driven by the thought of freedom,
Flying on the wings of exhilaration,
Slowly into the distance now,
Into the future,
She races on.

Sally Paul (13) Broadwater School

Creatures

An Autumn walk in the wood
Twigs crack underfoot
Like sudden gunshots
In the empty air
Squirrels, bleary-eyed with sleep,
Yet bright and alive
Hunt for their stores
And scamper away
At my footstep
Naked winter trees rustle
As birds take wing
In a whirr of sound
Soaring into the sky
Free
I want to run to leap and shout
To be free too

But I control myself
And walk quietly on.

Melanie Brough (13) Broadwater School

The Cat

Slinkily stepping
Out into the crisp
Cool air,
Its eyes
Pools of green
Pinpointed with black
The lady of the night.

A black fur coat
Ripples over
The fine contained body
Soft 'slipper'-padded feet
Tread carefully
Over the splintered fence
A whipping serpent
Controlling her balance.

A swift glide
Into the air
A landing of sophistication
Home to her territory.

Elizabeth Barnett (14) Broadwater School

The Little Creatures

'Right then class 9L1 today we are going to have an animal talk.'
'You mean creatures.'
'Yes if you like that Joe.'
'But I don't.'
'Just sit down and call it what you want Sam,
Does your watch have to keep playing 'All things bright and
beautiful'?'
'But it's got creatures in it Miss.'
'Yes I do know I was young once, anyway Mrs Smith is coming in.'
'She's fat!'
'What did you say . . . Sam please stop.'
'I like creatures I live with three of them.'
'And what are those Jasmin?'
'My Mummy, my Daddy and my brother.'
'Now that's not nice.'
'Miss, Miss.'
'Now what Paul?'
'I've gone to the toilet Miss.'
'Go to the office, mind the patch, that's Mrs Smith, be on your best
behaviour,
Sam, stop your watch.'

Naomi Elizabeth Sadler (14) Broadwater School

Creatures of the Night

Perched up on a branch he sits,
A watchful eye he keeps,
His 'hoot calls out - 'All is well',
To creatures of the night.

She shuffles in the fallen leaves
To find herself a bed,
But danger sensed, spines protect,
From creatures of the night.

Grey as the night his camouflage,
Except his white striped face,
Which peeps around his burglars mask,
A creature of the night.

Marion E McCabe (14) Broadwater School

Girl in Bright Colours

Nestled in the arms
Of a familiar figure,
Crouched in a homely doorway,
The confident, bright colours
Of the small girl
Search for glamour,
Clashing with the old man's own clothes
Of reserved, natural tones.
Secure, affectionate arms
Clamp her to his chest,
Protection from what the world has in store.
Penetrating glass beads
See only the light of life
From under her rich hair,
Flowing like a river
Straight from the ravines
Round the old man's eyes;
Signs of a life full of cheer,
The smooth fullness of a young skin,
A glow from within, like a flame in the depths of night.

Laura Bazley (15) Broadwater School

Tiger

Tiger roaring tiger brave.
His muscular jaws like a widening cave.
Chasing gazelles through the elephant grass.
When tiger runs he runs fast.
Taking the gazelle with the greatest of ease.
Tiger stands proud, satisfied, thankful and pleased.
Flesh through to bone the tiger does gorge.
Blood dripping from his pearly white claws.
Scavengers come to collect the remains.
Tiger sees them off, their loss his gain.
Tigers weight increases by day.
On the bare jungle floor he slaughters and slays.
Through the fauna melt his stripes of jet black.
As he beats once more his well worn track.

James Windless (13) Broadwater School

The Beaver

Furry little water species
Living in the forest
Feeding on the thistles
Shoots, bark and plants.

Swimming in the lake
With his head above the water
Slapping his spatulate tail
To keep himself afloat.

With his heavy built body, small ears and
Large blunt muzzled head
Living in his lodges
One day he will be dead.

Building dams digging holes
Scuttling here and there
He can gnaw through trees
With his jutting incisors.

Swimming in the marshes
Paddling on and on
Keeping warm with his furry coat
The beaver carries on.

Danny Ranger (14) Broadwater School

Medusa

She sits . . .
In the temple . . .
Surrounded by an icy tableau . . .
Played by actors centuries dispatched . . .
By her gaze of stony death.
Their blue and grey tones remind her . . .
Of long ago . . . in the temples . . .
Of mount Olympus . . .

She cries granite tears . . .
Which smash on contact with the steely floor . . .
As her scaly locks sway rhythmically . . .
In a comic dance . . .
To mock her.

Tim Jones (14) Broadwater School

Pigs

Pigs are pink,
You must believe,
Pigs are too nice to want to deceive.

Pigs have noses,
There is no doubt,
Every single pig has a snout.

Pigs are dirty,
I'm not denying,
They spend all day in thick mud lying.

Pigs are fat
It's plain to see,
You never see a pig as thin as can be.

Pigs are great,
Pigs are cool,
Pigs are my favourite animals of all.

Claire Etherton (14) Broadwater School

The Otter

Sleek, skilful and fast.
Flying like a missile through the years,
Like lightning on a stormy night,
Viscious, he knows he has his right.

A carnivore looking for his prey,
A silver glint, a pause, silent as he lay,
Then with one powerful flick of his tail
He makes the shimmering fish look like a snail.

Kerry Louise Hudson (13) Broadwater School

Jack

Jack walks through life
With his back bent double
Under the weight of years
His wrinkles mapping the flow
Of ancient rivers; traversing the
Furrows of his face
By a blind ploughman
Named Time
Memories sail through his mind
Bringing a tear or a smile
No regrets shatter his fragile form
Into sadness and pain
Like a china plate
Dropped from the Heart of life
British blood runs
Through his veins winding like a river
His hair dulled grey by age
Drifts slothlike from his scalp
As the days pass
Jack - old as the hills
A Peace and Calm

Neal Roberts (16) Onslow St Audrey School

A Riot

There was a *hush*
Then it happened
One shout
Heaved to the Heavens
Forcing me off my feet
Bodies shot out
Being trampled
Like a wall of flesh
Bodies slammed against me
I tried to scramble
But I fell to the sidewalk
Hundreds of swinging clubs
Coming towards me
Then as though
A rubber band had been cut
The sidewalk exploded
Policemen on horseback
Keeping back the roaring waves
And the sightless mob

(Poem based on an extract from 'The Friends' by Rosa Guy)

Louise Roberts (16) Onslow St Audrey School

Rain Destruction

Low, dark, dull,
Lifeless anvil clouds.
Amalgamate in the skies.
Suddenly without warning
The shapes unleash their attack:
Bombardment of rain, sleet and hail.

Grass: drowning, suffocating
In the grey dissolution.
Plants: bent double under the
Strain of the raging wraith rain
Dead leaves pulverised into mulch.
The once dry earth, now churned into mud.

Animals flee for any form of shelter.
Birds retreat:
Their feathers saturated.
Ponds and pools mixed into turmoil
By the pounding; water overflows the edges.

The final blow occurs: a low
Distant rumble.
A crescendo of sound.
The clap of thunder rolls across the sky.
The darkness is cracked in two.
Water submerges the land.

Que Lu (17) Onslow St Audrey School

The Long Cold Autumn

The cold wind bites and numbs your nose
The lonely road sound of silence.
Out of the woods whispered echoes
After gales the sun cowers
A long wave goodbye until the summer
Rain is dampening the trees
The old wood with nothing
Trees whisper echoes
November, the last of the summer.

Eve Jessica Elizabeth See (14) Onslow St Audrey School

An Absent Friend

The pale winter sun had begun its descent
The icy afternoon that I saw you there.
The gnarled black view of the aged elm
Seemed to grow against the chilly gloam.

For just one moment I saw you
Milk white skin and frail of figure.
A slight shape silhouetted against
The fading light.

'Can't catch me!' - did I hear you say
Or was it a ghost of a memory
A wisp of a life long past
Carried through the dusk by a cruel wind?

Or was it the crow, calling
From its perch on one black arm?
Could it be you, my beloved
Or just nature's games being played once more.

Christine Horton (17) Onslow St Audrey School

The Mill

The tattered old mill on the banks of the river
holds many a secret inside,
of lonely old travellers; ghosts in the night,
who have roamed alone far and wide.

Many phantoms have strayed and ventured within
to rest their weary head.
Only the mill knows the reason why
they have chosen this place for their bed.

These travellers visit through all kinds of weather,
in fog, rain and snow.
Only the mill knows why they come,
and the mill only knows why they go.

Wendy Knox (17) Onslow St Audrey School

The Church

Before; morning rays shone through glass stained,
Projecting beams of light through the holiness
surround,
The sacred house filled with voices strained,
Walls echoing with hallowed sound.

People, O, people, so many; a memory
Seated, pewed, standing alike, they all were,
Waiting just waiting for the ceremony,
Eyes darting heads turning welcoming her.

But for what duration did those blessed vows last,
Gazing now towards that place once so holy
Derelict now like me and my past,
This decaying sanctuary, making life so lowly.

Stones now grey forming crumbling remains,
The isle, once marvelled at, now detested,
It's marbled floor cracked like those windows once
stained,
Memories now rife, here for years have rested.

The ruins, the dust, an empty home,
Emphasise more my love sadly removed,
From myself my person, but memories not,
Company now an epitaph on an old grey stone.

Elizabeth Darton (17) Onslow St Audrey School

No One Cares

The cattle continued to eat,
Yet the world stood still,
The sky moved in a colourless sheet,
As I said my farewell.

The stark trees melancholy wave,
With cascading arms,
Reaching down towards the grave,
Beckoning the spirit,
To transcend its earthly way.

I know the scene from my childhood dreams,
The never ending spirals of memories,
Moved together, in my heart;
Thus to allow me to part;
From she loved one, deep below;
She may be dead, yet no one knows.

Dawn Rutherford (17) Onslow St Audrey School

Child of '93

What was she thinking? Nobody knew,
As she sat in her pushchair in everyone's view.
What was she seeing? Her eyes crystal clear
Her vision unclouded, with little to fear.

Safe, warm and comfy, of worries had none,
Would sit quite contented all day in the sun.
Spread over with sun-cream, she didn't know why,
Hadn't heard of the holes growing over the sky.

She loved it at teatime, in front of the box,
Fed bits of animals followed by chocs.
She gurgled at 'Play Days' and laughed at the news,
And screamed when the President spoke of his views.

She smiled at the pictures of faraway wars,
Didn't notice humanity in its own jaws.
So what are her prospects born into this mess?
Can strong love be nurtured, the balance redressed?

She hasn't been christened, I don't know her name.
She's still young and innocent, thinks life's a game.
But she's a child of the future, what more can we ask,
Than she sets her heart to it and succeeds with her task.

Sally-Ann Spencer (17) Parmiters School

Wind

I battle my way through the open park.
Gushing, howling, the whistling wind
Scorches my face, bites my ears and scratches my eyes.

I see children, clinging to parents.
They seem frightened and so scared.
The wind is like an inhuman monster trying to kidnap them,
Take them away from the people they love.

I continue my battle.
I am out of breath yet still I haven't reached the end of the park.
I will continue to fight the wind, to reach my destination.
I will not let it win.

The wind becomes fiercer like a child in a temper,
Viciously picking up armfuls of dead, dried leaves,
Tossing them into my path.
They whirl and twist like a roller-coaster,
Crashing into me like angry bats hitting me with iron wings.

At last I reach the end of the park,
And gratefully take shelter in a doorway.

Stacey Higgs (16) The Bedwell School

What Man Has Marred

A solitary seagull gave forth its haunting cry
to the swell below
The cry echoed against the rugged weather-beaten cliffs
Carried there silently by the pure breeze
and then it came
A black death
Stealthily creeping, engulfing all,
showing no mercy
A hideous intruder disgorging its cargo to the swell
powerless to resist
and reluctantly urging it onwards
towards the shore
The air, heavy with the stench of death
chokes the seagull's cry
and the silence reflects yet another disaster
to shipwreck our hopes of man
in harmony with nature

Mary Woodland (14) Presdales School

Bosnia

The child stares
Silently, so silently
As his father goes out, into the danger
To fight his neighbour
and he wonders why

The child listens
Intently, so intently
As the ring of gunfire, and bombs
Echoes in his ears
and he wonders why

The child watches
Sadly, so sadly
As his mother weeps at the news of his father
The man he will never see again
and he wonders why

On the other side of the world, we watch
Safely and securely
As the people starve
Weak and helpless
and we wonder . . . why?

Sarah Ashton Bartlett (15) Presdales School

Time

I am ongoing
and run lives
My hands rule the world
You can fight against me
But I always win
I sit on walls
And rest on wrists
I am days and weeks
and months and years
Nothing can stop my power
Births and deaths are my doing
Man wishes me away
and then wishes me back
but neither works
I am the beginning
and the end
I bring happiness
and sadness
I am eternity

Emma Phipps (14) Presdales School

Waiting for Death

As the wind blew unmercifully
Through the trenches
A frozen darkness hung around
With a nip as sharp as a snake's bite
It was colder than ice
It was numbingly cold
The rain was beating down
Bruising the ground
The blood and mud river
Forming death's tributaries
The wind too strong to fight against

Hidden behind mud and sand banks
Men lay waiting for death
Poised to pounce for Glory
Thoughts running riot
Then . . . the heart stopping sound
The death tune played
Faces drained to white
Hearts stopped beating
Honour took over and moved forward to attack
Then the sound again, but louder
Coming nearer
The guns . . .
They had no aim
The bullets just searched for blood
They thrived on it
They found the taut flesh
They leaked the pain

Then from somewhere came a shadow
It was dark, but *it* was darker
It covered the soldier
The soldier was dead

There was no hope for the brave
There is no place for war

Estelle Hornsby (15) Presdales School

Watching Them Waiting

You settle down to watch TV
With your food upon your knee
The television goes on
A picture springs to the screen
You change the channel
You turn a blind eye
To what you don't want to see
To the pictures of starving people

You are now safely watching a comedy
But the pictures still haunt you
At the back of your mind
They won't go away
You still see the children
So thin and ill
And the mothers' pleading eyes
Crying to the world for help

Where did we go wrong?
How can it be that we waste so much
While our brothers starve
They know nothing of fast cars and TV
All they know is the horrible reality of death
Surely we must strive to change this
To bring hope to the starving
And peace of mind for all

Victoria Swaile (15) Presdales School

Watching and Waiting

Watching and waiting
Forever it seems
Looking at the world rushing by
With places to go, things to do
Except me, on the sideline, viewing
all to see
Watching and waiting for my time to come
To be up there in Paradise
Watching and waiting
As dismal winter trudges into the
miracle of spring, and as summer
turns into the beautiful colours of Autumn
When will it all end? I wonder
When will it all end?
Watching and waiting
Feeling my soul drifting away
My time is coming, I can feel it
It won't be long now.

Ann Marie Pollard (15) Presdales School

The Story of Life

The story of life is quicker
than the wink of an eye
Death is an inspiration for the soul
Is it really the end?
Find salvation in your dreams
For craziness in Heaven
I hear you say as I fade away
The story of love is hello and goodbye
Until we meet again . . .

Lucy Griffiths (15) Presdales School

Bubbles

Pop! Another one disappears off the face of this world
Rainbows encased in crystal spheres
Shining brightly like small sunbeams
Bubbles last but a few moments
Floating through the air with the grace of a ballerina
Weighing less than an owl's feather
Colourful stained glass in a newly-washed window
or perhaps these soapy birds
are really enchanted pools who
Pop! Return to their masters or mistresses
Who they have missed so much
During their seconds of gliding in the air

Joanna Winterton (14) Presdales School

Clouds

Clouds.
Shapeless objects,
travelling the skies without a meaning.
Greyness,
spreading for eternity,
like white paint misting clear water,
closing our world in,
forming a dreary barrier
between us and the light.
Clouds.
The wispy nothingness
creates distorted shapes and figures.
In winter,
a forecast of rain,
scudding across the dark canopy.
And, after the downpour,
between the newly-washed clouds,
glistening sun sparkles over the world.

Ellen Laura Morgan (14) Presdales School

Ending

With a gurgling cry, the stream runs dry;
This is the end of all hope.
And the church bells chime the forbidden time,
Yes, this is the end of all hope.

The sun's angry glare heats the stuffy air;
This is the end of all life.
With steamy dew on the battered yew,
Yes, this is the end of all life.

Nobody tried to keep our planet alive;
This is the end of the world.
Yet everyone knew that their time was due,
Yes, this is the end of the world.

Catherine Stevenson (14) Presdales School

A Place of Dreams

There she sits,
The dim cave lit only by
Pots and pots of bright, bubbling liquids,
Sparkling, shimmering,
As is her face as she thoughtfully mixes the concoctions,
Rosy cheeks aglow.
The thick walls lined with shelves,
Of jars and jars of sweet-smelling herbs and spices,
Tins of candies,
Bottles of clear, sparkling oils,
Held tight by small, brown corks,
Little bags of unimaginable magics,
Wishing pearls,
Coloured powders, like dust, merge together.
Bubbles drift lazily about the room,
Bursting casually and showering gold all around,
Like gentle, coloured rain,
The potions prepared with such kindness,
Upon the old, wooden table,
Such care put into each,
As each is unique,
For you and you alone,
For this is the place where night thoughts are born,
This is the Place of Dreams.

Lucy Guilford (15) Presdales School

My Place of Dreams

The sun blazing on the horizon,
The breeze coming in from across the sea.
The golden sand beneath my feet,
As I stroll along in the summer's heat.

My long hair blowing in the wind,
The waves lapping up against my feet.
The gulls are circling high above,
As my mind dreams of the things I love.

The sand stretching out as far as the eye can see,
Not a soul in sight to disturb my thoughts.
I have no worries in this enchanted scene,
And I know I'll return to this place of dreams.

Sarah Purkis (14) Presdales School

Day to Night

A tinge of scarlet above the dark, silhouetted skyline
illuminating the milkman's humming, the first birds calling,

The crimson light of dawn, flooding the horizon with glowing colour,

Harsh, white rays of sun glinting off the early morning
frost, rising from a warm bed, to the smell of bacon,

And the day moves on . . .

Deep azure skies of midmorning, enveloping the Earth
like a mantle, wispy clouds like discarded pillows.

The hushed white light of noon, a bright disc of
brilliant yellow intensity sits high in the sky.

Wearied faces and tired limbs signal that the day is
wearing thin and already the sun has begun its descent.

Already the shadows are lengthening, the sun is touching
the horizon. Warm fires and crumpets, oozing with butter and jam.

The sun once more has returned to the edge. The sky turns
a mottled colour of purples, oranges and reds.

Grey dusk. The sun has once more dipped its head below
the dark skyline. Trees are no more than silhouettes
against the dimming backdrop of sky.

The vast expanse of ebony-black nothingness, blotting out
the day, replacing it with shimmering, lustrous stars.

Peter John Abbott (15) Fearnhill School

I Would Paint

I would paint
All the hugs in the world
For the children that need them
All the care that they want
I would paint food to feed them.

The homes that they need,
Love for all different races
I'd paint the clothes and warmth
And the smiles on their faces.

I would paint
The first laugh in the world
The first smile, the first giggle,
The first chuckle or bellow
I would paint the first tickle.

I'd paint, all the happiness in the world
I'd paint peace on the earth
I'd paint loving and caring
And I'd paint the first birth.

I'd paint swimming and diving,
Breaststroke, front crawl
Somersaults, backflips,
I'd paint the first fall.

I'd paint all the colours,
The reds and the blue,
I'd paint everyone in the world
Just as happy as me and you.

Eleanor F Haigh (13) Fearnhill School

Caravan Holiday

I open one eye,
is it time for school?
Where am I? What's that?
I hear the sounds of birds.
And then I know
I am on holiday.

I slide open the door
peep through the gap.
Anyone up yet?
Dad's gone for a jog
my sister's asleep
I wonder where we will go today.

I love our caravan
so warm and snug
its green velvet curtains
and the smell of wood
here on my bunk
I sit and wait.

Debra Prince (12) Townsend School

The Whale

As it glides through the water slow and graceful.
You wouldn't think it was that heavy.
The sunlight reflects on its back
the dark shadow beneath.
The cries sound so ghostly echoing from
deep waters.
Cries, haunting cries of what - happiness, sadness, help
who knows?
When it comes to the surface
for a breath of air
anything could be up there.
Ships could be waiting getting their harpoons ready
tourists crammed on little boats waiting to
take photos.
Beware!
Memories may be all that's left of
this creature.

Hannah Laws (12) Townsend School

Tongue Twisters

I'm gonna tell you tongue twisters
And if you don't like them sonny
Go and get them out of a book
They've gotta be funny.

A tree toad loved a tree toad
That lived up in a tree.
She was a three toed tree toad,
But a two toed three toad was he.

Betty Batter had some butter
But she said this butter's bitter.
If I bake this bitter butter,
It will make my batter bitter.

Fanny fetter found a fan,
A fan found Fanny Fetter.
But Fanny Fetter lost her tan
And wept till she felt better.

Lee John Browning (13) Townsend School

Death

Death!
Death is like a huge pit, never ending,
Death!
Death is like an unknown book, not knowing
when something's going to happen,
Death!
Death is like nothingness, wandering through
space,
Death!

Adili Muguro (12) North Wesminster School

The Woods

The shady untroubled woods
Are quiet and still,
Not a bird sang
Nor a hedgehog snuffle.

The rays of sunlight
Caught the branches of the trees,
The birds begin
Their sweet and joyful song.

A hedgehog shuffles
Across the golden brown leaves,
A grey squirrel leaps and bounds
From branch to branch.

This place which was quiet and still
Is also the peaceful environment for wildlife,
We should leave it as it is
And never let it be disturbed.

Clare Forder (14) George Abbot School

My Bug

My bug lay still and does not speak,
Has two spots and one thin streak.
Lifeless he looks as though asleep,
He will not murmur or dare to creep.
For him to live his life outdoors,
He must stave off the predators.
Food for our bug is hard to find,
He forages at times, almost half blind.
In those long and endless tunnels,
Exploring new exciting funnels,
In his quest and true endeavour,
A morsel, a crumb he must discover.
Not only for our bug to survive,
More food will keep the young alive,
There may be two or three or four,
Each mite to be cared for.

Lucy Taylor (13) Thamesmead School